MW00628009

CouRaGeous

Cuentos

A Journal of Counternarratives

A Journal of the Department of Critical

Race, Gender & Sexuality Studies

Cal Poly Humboldt

Arcata, California

The Press at Cal Poly Humboldt

© Department of Critical Race, Gender & Sexuality Studies

Cal Poly Humboldt

1 Harpst Street

Arcata, CA 95521-8299

Chapter images created by the Corageous Cuentos staff

ISBN 978-1-947112-95-7

About This Journal

CouRaGeouS Cuentos is a journal publication by the Department of Critical Race, Gender & Sexuality Studies (CRGS) at Cal Poly Humboldt. The journal is available both in digital commons at: digitalcommons. humboldt.edu/courageouscuentos/ and as a printed, bound copy available through Amazon.com.

The works published in this journal are by students who took the course *Ethnic Studies 107: Chican@/Latinx Lives; CRGS 331: Radical Futures: Race, Environment, and Social Justice;* and students in the Promotorx Transformative Educators Program. Together, students want to make their stories, their counternarratives, available to their families, their communities, and any other students who could relate to their experiences.

The journal is published annually by students in the spring semester of each calendar year. The editing of the works is a collective effort by students in the class, students in *Ethnic Studies 280: Courageous Cuentos Production,* and the instructor of *Ethnic Studies 107: Chican@/Latinx Lives.* Every student in the class has the opportunity to publish their work and do so on a voluntary basis. Some students submit more than one entry, in addition to visual art that reflects central themes in each year's submissions.

Land & Labor Acknowledgement

As a student journal at HSU, we would like to acknowledge that HSU sits on the land of the Wiyot peoples which includes the Wiyot Tribe, Bear River Rancheria, and Blue Lake Rancheria. Arcata is known as Goudi'ni meaning "over in the woods" or "among the redwoods." Wiyot peoples continue to remain in relationship to these lands through ceremony, culture, and stewardship. They are important parts of not only the history of this area but also in continuing knowledges of this place.

We encourage those in Wiyot territory to make a contribution to the <u>Honor Tax</u> (http://honortax.org/), a system set up by local non-native people as one way to recognize and respect the sovereignty of the Wiyot people. Though there is no similar system for other Tribes in the region, we encourage direct giving to Tribes and Native-led efforts.

You can support such efforts on our campus by supporting the Native American Studies Department and the NAS Food Sovereignty Lab (nasp.humboldt.edu/fsl). Take their courses, attend their programming, and support their community projects and events.

We would also like to do a labor acknowledgement and recognize and acknowledge the labor upon which our country, state, and institutions are built. Remember that our country is built on the labor of enslaved people who were kidnapped and brought to the US from the African Continent and recognize the continued contribution of their survivors. We acknowledge all immigrant labor, including voluntary, involuntary, and trafficked peoples who continue to serve within our labor force.

Reconocimiento de Tierras y Labor

Nos gustaría reconocer que la Universidad Estatal de Humboldt se encuentra en la tierra de los pueblos Wiyot que incluye la Tribu Wiyot, Bear River Rancheria y Blue Lake Rancheria. Arcata se conoce como Goudi'ni, que significa "en el bosque" o "entre las secuoyas". Los pueblos Wiyot continúan manteniendo una relación con estas tierras a través de la ceremonia, la cultura y la administración. Son partes importantes no solo de la historia de esta área, sino también de los conocimientos continuos de este lugar.

Alentamos a quienes se encuentran en el territorio de Wiyot a hacer una contribución al impuesto al honor (http://honortax.org/), un sistema establecido por personas no nativas locales como una forma de reconocer y respetar la soberanía del pueblo de Wiyot. Aunque no existe un sistema similar para otras tribus en la región, alentamos las donaciones directas a las tribus y los esfuerzos dirigidos por los nativos.

Puede apoyar tales esfuerzos en nuestro campus apoyando al Departamento de Estudios Nativos Americanos y al Laboratorio de Soberanía Alimentaria de NAS (nasp.humboldt.edu/fsl). Realice sus cursos, asista a su programación y apoye sus proyectos y eventos comunitarios.

También nos gustaría hacer un reconocimiento y agradecer (y reconocer) la labor con la que (cual) nuestro país, estado, e instituciones fueron construidas. Recordemos que nuestro país fue construido con la labor de personas esclavizadas quienes fueron secuestrados y traídos a los Estados Unidos desde el continente Africano y reconocemos las contribuciones continuadas de sus sobrevivientes. Reconocemos todo trabajo hecho por inmigrantes, incluyendo voluntario, involuntario, y personas traficadas quienes continúan sirviendo dentro de nuestra fuerza laboral.

Acknowledgements

We would like to express our gratitude to all the writers who submitted their stories—from students taking ES 107: Chican@/Latinx Lives; CRGS 331: Radical Futures: Race, Environment and Social Justice; and ES 310: The U.S. & Mexico Border taught by Dr. Nancy Pérez in CRGS, to Eureka High School and Arcata High School students who participated in workshops led by Dr. Marisol Ruiz and the PromotorX Transformative Educators program. We would like to thank two high school teachers who graciously shared their classroom with us: Tim Olson at Eureka High school and Anayeli Auza at Arcata High School. We would also like to thank the PromotorX students who helped teach about a pedagogy of healing, and guided youth to produce their healing texts for this volume: Georgina Cerda Salvarrey, Namixtu'lu Esteva, Griselda Valdez, Carmen Sahagun, Chelsea Rios Gomez, Arianna Bucio, Joahnna Tool, Athens Marrón, Elizabeth Rubio, Michael Steelman and Abraham Neri.

Many thanks to the students in the CouRaGeouS Cuentos Production class of 2023 for continuing the vision of the journal of publishing students' counternarratives. We appreciate your hard work and dedication in editing the submissions, designing the journal, and organizing our annual CouRaGeouS Cuentos Celebration Event. You created a celebration for students and the community where they felt safe and empowered to read and feel inspired by each other's writings and art.

Special thanks to Digital Scholarship Librarian Kyle Morgan for the assistance with promoting our journal and for inviting us to connect with the larger published writers' community on campus. Kyle, thank you for always checking in on us, and of course for putting in the last final details to our journal before it goes to print. We appreciate you so much! This journal would not be possible without you.

Much love and appreciation to our campus photographer, Kellie Jo Brown, for visiting us early in the semester to take photos of our production team. Your photographs have allowed us to begin a visual archive of our work on this campus and the students leading and growing the journal along the way. Your thoughtfulness and attentiveness created a safe, fun, and comfortable space for us to feel loved and seen.

To the staff and faculty of the Department of Critical Race, Gender & Sexuality Studies: Dr. Ramona Bell, Dr. Christina Hsu Accomando, Dr. Paul Michael Atienza, Dr. Roberto Monico, Professor Maral Attallah, Professor Ana Bernal, Professor Rain Marshall, Dr. Janet Winston, and Jasmin Torres. We would also like to give a huge thank you to the Cal Poly Humboldt Ethnic Studies Council for sponsoring our swag, and to Sandra Brekke for providing staff support when we needed it the most. Thank you to Dean Jeffrey Crane for also supporting our journal.

To the DHSI Grant from the School of Education for co-sponsoring the CouRaGeouS Cuentos Release Event and the printing of the posters and journals for students. Thank you to the Creando Raíces team for your continued support of the journal and its vital role at this university.

CouRaGeouS Cuentos Production Spring 2023

Dr. Nancy Pérez, Assistant Professor
Critical Race, Gender & Sexuality Studies

Dr. Marisol Ruiz, Associate Professor
School of Education & Promotorx Transformative Educators

Managing Editor
Audriana Peñaloza

Editors

Xitlaly De La Torre Canchola
Noemi Gonzalez Maldonado
Chelsea Ríos Gómez

Art & Book Design

Esteban Langarica
Eduardo A. Moreno-Ortiz
Maria Citlalli Rodriguez

Social Media & Event Marketing

Dillon Avery Harp
Daniel Garcia
Brianna R. Juarez

Writing Fellow

Victoria Olsen

Table of Contents

Land & Labor Acknowledgement   v
Acknowledgements   vi
CouRaGeouS Cuentos Production Spring 2023   ix
Introduction: CouRaGeouS Cuentos as a Site of Spirit
Protection and Restoration
Nancy Pérez and Marisol Ruiz   xv

Chapter One: Otoño: Fall

Mi Lugar Favorito
Anilu Rodriguez   2

Aprender a Vivir
Emmanuel Caro Montoya   3

Dejandolo Todo
Luis Francisco Martínez   4

Chicana, Para El Norte
Kacie E. Figueroa   5

Ama
Arianna Bucio   6

Deseo Poder Conocerte
Hansell Vásquez   8

**Al Caer La Noche
La Mariposa Desvanece**
Nayali Abarca   10

enough.
Carmen Sahagun   11

Gracias a Dios
Carmen Benavides-Garb   13

Gregorio Muniz (x3)
Gregorio Muniz   15

I am Not Afraid
Karen Zurita   17

La Major Medicina
Marco Antonio Cruz
Hernandez   18

My Debt
Valeria Ruiz   19

Naypyidaw
Matt Aung   20

Necesidad y Sacrificio: San Ysidro, Su Frontera, y Su Gente
Anitza Monarrez   21

Interviews   22

The Healing Words of Nature
Sky Kili   27

Una Vida Sin Mamá y Hermanos
Luis Eduardo Rodriguez   28

Where Am I From?
By Kimberli Pacheco   29

Unlearn
Georgina Cerda Salvarrey   30

Desaprender
Georgina Cerda Salvarrey   31

Chapter Two: Invierno: Winter

Dejar Todo Sin Dejar Nada
Andrea Itzel Velazco Quiroz   34

Luna Sleeping
Nayali Abarca   35

Dejar a Mis Padres
Luis Camacho Garcia   36

Basil & Rose
Covin Sigala   37

Descubriendo
Joahnna Tool   38

How Riverside County Celebrates Historical Indigenous Oppression
Logan Roselli   39

La Madrugada Amarga
Gerber Campos   44

Untitled (Mess No. 1)
Jesse Morales   46

Juntes (Ode to In Lak'ech)
Marisol Ruiz, Griselda Valdez, Mayra Meza, and Georgina Cerda Salvarrey   47

Mi Recuerdo Inolvidable
Jose Maceda   48

Miedo
Griselda Valdez, Mayra Meza, and Gina Cerda Salvarrey   49

Nuestros Pasos En Algo Diferente
Christo Santiago   50

Ode to the One That Raised Me
Chelsea Rios Gomez   51

Mis Placas Tectónicas: La Culpa, La Tristeza y El Coraje
Tim Olson   52

Four-Leafed Clovers
Audriana Peñaloza   54

Our People
Dillon Avery Harp   56

Be Proud and Loud
Sydney Leland   59

The Aftermath of Absence
Jordan Lavant and
Haley Fedalizo   60

**The Maidu and Miwok
People in the Wake of
California's "Growth"**
Benjamin Cross   61

Walnuts
Anonymous   65

The Places We're From
Nico Chorny and Matt Aung   66

**Una Vida Sin Mi Mamá en
Otro País**
Miriam Rodriguez   67

**A Testimony Denouncing
Religion**
Kena Arnold-Malufau   72

Mejillas Rosadas
Kathryn Lozano   74

Cambios en 1...2 por 3
Anayka Flores Olguin   75

La Pantalla
Angel Martinez Toribio   76

Locked
Yami E.P.M.   77

Body is Soil, Hair is Flower
Minerva Torres   78

My Garden
By Mia Rose Rios   79

My Mother the Spider
Hunter Circe   80

Leslie & Poppy
Leslie Burkhart   85

Silencio
Noemi Gonzalez Maldonado   86

Sueños / Dreams
Adrian Vielma Garcia   89

Radical Futures
Isabela Escobedo   91

Xelfi
Namixtu'lú' Esteva   96

Chapter Three: Primavera: Spring

Somos Músicos
Davis Boone y Mayra Meza   70

Agradecida
Kimberlyn Moreno   71

Understanding My New Normal
Brianna Juarez 97

Kathy Pero Like Katí
Kathy Zamora 100

Rooted Home
Olie M. Espinoza 102

Para Mi Papa, Que Sigue Viviendo En El Mar
Melissa Torres Escalante 103

Chapter Four: Verano: Summer

Up River Coyote
Emmanuel Pihneefich Cyr 108

agua bendita
Jessica Aguirre 112

Our Connection
By Maria Citlalli Rodriguez 117

The Puzzle of Me
Matt Aung 122

Fruit Salad
Nayali Abarca 123

Summer: An Accordion Poem
Kyra Alway and Paolo Bosques-Paulet 124

Rosa Parks
Isabella Garcia Figueroa 125

Remembering My Home
Brittany Arzola 126

Por Mi
Destiny Rodriguez 131

Our Need for Space
Alicia Lopez 133

No Effect on Me
Brenda Santos 138

Mis Motivadores
Eduardo A. Moreno-Ortiz 139

¡Viva México!
Diego Vega and Georgina Cerda Salvarrey 141

I Am Who I Am
Claudia Lopez-Hernandez 142

I am
Kyra Alway 143

Here We Stand
Nelsy Ramirez Pacheco and Chelsea Rios Gomez 144

From Roots to Wings
Anonymous, Anonymous 145

El Primer Dia
Erick Esparza 146

Nopayele
Cayele Ameyalli Esteva   147

**Being Part of the LGBTQ+
Community**
Genevive Cerda   148

Querida Niña
Georgina Cerda Salvarrey   149

This is Me
Kimberly Piñon   150

The Language of English
Sasha Ortiz Bazan   151

Volume 6 Poster Design   **153**
Paleta Recipe
Brianna R. Juarez   **154**
Author Bios   **155**

Introduction:
CouRaGeouS Cuentos as a Site of
Spirit Protection and Restoration

Nancy Pérez and Marisol Ruiz

We wanted this volume to focus on healing texts because we were inspired by the work of Anita Tijerina Revilla, who wrote "Attempted Spirit Murder: Who Are Your Spirit Protectors and Your Spirit Restorers?" Her work reminded us that education *spirit murders* us. She defines *spirit murder* as racist, classist, sexist, homophobic, trans-phobic, anti-immigrant, ableist, and/or ageist traumas experienced in educational settings that have the power to spiritually and emotionally destroy our dreams and our desires to exist. It silences our voices, it erases our stories and our bodies from the literature, histories and her-stories. She reminds us of how we can protect our community by being spirit restorers and protectors. According to Tijerina, spirit restorers and protectors are "people, places, organizations, beliefs, and/or practices (they can also be art, poetry, books, music, and dance) that give marginalized people the strength to reject and survive attempted spirit murder and/or restore our wounded spirits, especially in the face of repeated attacks and woundings both inside and outside of in-stitutions of education" (2021, 39). We want Courageous Cuentos to be that site of spirit protection and restoration for all of those who have been silenced and erased by their discipline/s. Courageous Cuentos is that space where we share our stories that help uplift us. The stories in this volume remind us that the healing process is complex and looks differently for each one of us. Some of us are beginning the healing journey by acknowledging our pain and scars, some are in the process of healing, and others have accepted where they are in their healing journey.

When we worked with the high schools, we made sure to use plantitas as medicine so they can use the spirit of the plants to protect them and remind them how the land loved them and continues to be there to protect and fortify our spirits. Lavender can heal our anxiety as we walk into a toxic environment. Even in these environments these stories help to serve as a means / space where we can restore ourselves. Healing is also acknowledging that we are not alone; these stories we share help to tell one another that these similar experiences are not about us; it is larger than us because they are the systems of oppression which try to destroy our spirits but together, we can heal, protect and restore our communities. We are a beautiful community. Our stories are vibrating together as one. This volume is an energy that wants to shield, protect and restore one another through our beautiful loving experiences. So, let's connect with one another as we read each other's writing. Let's read with the intention of healing. We would like to dedicate this poem to all the readers and writers of this edition of Courageous Cuentos.

Tú y yo
Sanemos
Juntos
Vamos a combinar nuestras energías
Y volvámonos uno
Sanemos, unamos nuestras almas,
Al compartir nuestras historias
Nuestras historias de amor, fuerza, y sanación
Sanemos y compartamos nuestras historias de dolor, tormento, estrés y angustia.
Sanemos y compartamos nuestras historias de placer, risas y alegría
Compartamos nuestros consejitos
Que hemos aprendido a lo largo del camino
Si, sanemos
Y compartamos un pedacito de nuestro corazón.
Un pedacito de quiénes somos
Que nuestras historias ayuden a iluminar cada rincón de este mundo
Sanemos mientras tu historia
ayuda a sanar mis cicatrices
ayuda a proteger mi alma y mi espíritu
Sanemos mientras nos alimentamos con los néctares de nuestras historias

Sanemos mientras leemos nuestras historias convirtiéndonos en gotas de agua alimentando nuestras raíces,
fortaleciendo nuestra comunidad
Sanemos para que las semillas de las escrituras florezcan en nuestras almas
Sanemos mientras guardamos cada historia sagradamente en nuestro corazón.

Chapter 1
Otoño : Fall

Mi Lugar Favorito
Anilu Rodriguez

Muchas veces nos dicen cómo comportarnos dependiendo del lugar en el que estamos. Si estás en una iglesia tienes que ser puro, divino y guardar silencio. Si estás en clase te sientes manso y otras veces hasta despistado, tienes que escuchar al maestro y participar de vez en cuando. Sin embargo, hay una sensación que es difícil de explicar, cuándo estás con tus seres queridos, cuando estás en el ahora y no te importa nada más. Yo creo que sería como cuando estás en un concierto de rock, sacudiéndote por todos lados, un sin duda magnánimo sentimiento, pues así me siento yo en mi lugar favorito, México.

Por algunas circunstancias, la vida me alejó de estos conciertos, me alejó del lugar que me vio crecer, me alejó por las oportunidades que este país me puede brindar, me alejó por el "sueño americano" el cuál solo me hizo sentir más segura si estaba callada, el cual solo me ensombreció. Pero en este camino me he prometido triunfar y todas estas experiencias me hicieron darme cuenta que estallar para encontrarme está bien, que para llegar a la cima también se tiene que batallar. Ahora sé que nadie nos puede silenciar y que no está tan mal cambiar los conciertos de vez en cuando para enfocarte, para descubrir, para trazar tu vida. Y aunque la vida me ha separado de mi lugar favorito, de alguna forma u otra siempre volvemos. Siempre lo llevo en mi corazón.

Aprender a Vivir
Emmanuel Caro Montoya

The kids in my class are talking to me.
"No les entiendo".
Es otro idioma diferente.

En mi casa nomás se habla español,
nada de inglés.

Quiero aprender inglés,
 ya aprendí el idioma,
 ahora, puedo hablar
con mis compañeros de clase.

Mis padres me hablan,
"What are they saying?"
Did I forget how to speak Spanish?
I can't communicate with my own parents.
I'm annoyed,
Frustrated.

¿Por qué no nos hablas hijo?
¿No sabes qué decir?

I'm going to learn Spanish,
so I can communicate with them again.

Dejandolo Todo
Luis Francisco Martínez

¿Has sentido que algo te aprieta en el pecho y que no te deja respirar? ¿Un nudo en la garganta que te aprieta fuerte que no puedes hablar? ¿Has tenido miedo de enfrentarte a esos sentimientos, pero te haces el fuerte para no verte débil frente a los demás? Pues eso es lo que yo he sentido.

Cuando me despedí de mi familia sentí que no podía respirar, pero el orgullo de ser un hombre comprimió esos sentimientos, para que no vieran lo débil que soy en lo profundo de mi ser. Dejar a mi familia, a mis amigos y a mis seres queridos fue algo duro, porque sabía que no los volvería a ver de nuevo, solo para tener una vida mejor. Pese a esa opción, estoy convencido que saben cómo me sentí en ese momento. Yo estoy convencido que tomé una buena decisión de venir y poder cumplir mis sueños.

Cuando me estaba despidiendo de mi mamá, la abracé fuerte y luego me llené de emociones que no pude dejar salir, por mi estúpido orgullo de hombre. Mi mamá rompió en llanto, porque sabía que no nos volvería a ver por un buen tiempo. Al igual que mi mamá, mi abuelita también rompió en llanto cuando me abrazó a mí y a mi hermano, por no volvernos a ver. Después de despedirme de mi familia; mi padre, mi hermano y yo nos fuimos de mi pueblo. Mi padre solo nos acompañó en el viaje hasta la frontera, nos la pasamos bien en el camino y todo, pero en el autobús que íbamos se le descompuso el aire acondicionado. Lo peor es que hacía mucho calor, el aire se sentía caliente y estar afuera del autobús era peor, porque te golpeaba una ráfaga de viento caliente y los fuertes rayos del sol caían sobre nosotros.

Al momento de cruzar la frontera no pudimos despedirnos de nuestro padre, porque nos pusimos nerviosos pensando en sí pasaríamos o no. Nos llevaron a un cuarto donde nos hicieron muchas preguntas, que no dio tiempo para despedirnos de nuestro padre. Yo volteé a ver a mi padre cuando nos estaban llevando, y en ese momento sentí que algo se rompió en mí, por no despedirme, porque gracias a él, estamos aquí cumpliendo nuestros sueños para poder tener una vida mejor. Yo estoy completamente agradecido con él y por eso le digo: gracias padre, gracias por todo.

Chicana, Para El Norte
Kacie E. Figueroa

I'm a CHICANA.

CHICANA: an American woman or girl of Mexican origin or descent.

CHi'känä/.

Mis padres migraron *para el norte* para la buena vida. Como dicen los gabachos el "American Dream." Built a family on Miwok land (Riverbank), where you can find the common, BUT NOT native, almond tree in the town's backyard. 1.5 million acres... 80% of the world's almond production is right in the heart of California's Central Valley, where this Chicana grew up.

Riverbank population 25,303. After high school graduation, ALMOST EVERYONE stayed in RBK. Why? Why stay? I said...

"FUCK IT! Voy *para el norte* — para Humboldt."

No one I know has ever been there; most people I know, have never gone so far up. The furthest they go is Santa Rosa or La Bahía. Most of my homeboys and hynas have never left RBK. I refuse to be that person and go to college at Stan State...NO. Riverbank, the Central Valley cannot own me. There isn't enough air to breathe here. Pollen and pollution has a chokehold on the Central Valley, with the highest allergy rate from late January to early November. All these almond orchards and still no fresh air. Some days it feels like la mierda de las vacas por la casa overrun my thoughts (it doesn't help that the train is around the corner). Yup, vamos pal norte (plus I heard it ACTUALLY RAINS).

Ama
Arianna Bucio

Ama,

desde que estaba chiquita,
 I always yearned to understand you.
I could never fathom
how you could love someone
who thought that fear
was synonymous with respect,
 y los golpes, sinónimos con el amor.
He constructed my idea of love,
con sus manos llenas de polvo y concreto.
I felt trapped
 in the house he built
Y mientras los años pasaban,
 el eco de sus gritos se quedaban
 dentro de estas paredes,
I sought refuge
 in the arms of a boy
que me pintaba un mundo
 lleno de rosas y sonrisas.
He tells me pretty words
when he doesn't make me cry
And when I do,
 he tells me
 I'm pretty.

Ama,
por primera vez,
 te entiendo.
I saw you
when I looked in the mirror
This twisted idea of love
 causing me to repeat
the same codependent cycle
I blamed you for.

Al fin,
 entendí lo que
era empatía
Y al perdonarte
por creer
que esto es todo
lo que el amor podría ser,
Me perdono
 a mí misma.

Deseo Poder Conocerte
Hansell Vásquez

Deseo poder verte y abrazarte. Esta vida sin ti se convierte en un infierno. Cada vez que voy creciendo me voy dando cuenta lo mucho que te extraño. Mi mente y mi corazón están en una gran batalla, porque mi mente quiere recordarte y mi corazón dice lo mucho que me duele recordarte.

Me duele saber que estoy creciendo sin ti, sin poder escuchar unos consejos tuyos. ¡Maldición! ¿por qué me toca a mí? me siento en mundos distintos.

No quiero seguir haciéndome más fuerte, porque cada vez que me piden hablar de ti, comienzo a llorar y me comienzo a debilitar.

Me duele saber los tantos años que he llorado por ti.

¡Encerrado en mi habitación queriendo recordar tu sonrisa, pero lo que gano es volver a llorar por ti!

Tanto quisiera que me pudieras ver, las metas que estoy logrando, y que me dijeras: "estoy orgulloso de ti hijo mío".

Ni cómo explicarle a la luna las tantas veces que te lloré. Quiero regresar a Guatemala para ver en dónde estás. Yo te necesito para toda la vida, créeme todo esto que estoy pasando es muy difícil.

Yo se que no soy el mejor hijo o el hijo que algún día deseaste.

Desde que tengo memoria, todos se burlaban de mí, tan solo por no tener a alguien que me protegiera. Todos me querían controlar, pero no sabían el daño que me estaban haciendo.

A mí me gusta escribir, pero yo sé que lo que escribo no es tan bueno, sin embargo es lo que me hace sentir quien soy, porque yo vivo en un mundo de tristeza y llanto.

Pero una cosa que voy a decir es que a pesar de todo lo que vivo, yo siempre te voy a querer y amar. Te lo promete tu hijo Hansel Yohaly Vasquez Moran.

Al Caer La Noche La Mariposa Desvanece
Nayali Abarca

enough.
Carmen Sahagun

words aren't enough
actions would've been
but in my moment of need
you chose to no longer want me.

everything fell on me
it came crashing down
on those evenings after school
he was there to protect us
to be the 'adult' in your stead
instead I found a monster
and now he forever lives
inside my head.

choosing to not chose
wasn't one of your options
it shouldn't have been hard
"mi niña querida"
that's what you used to call me...
until I showed you who he was.

faster than I could be afraid of it
the family was on his side
convinced they couldn't have
enabled the monster
hidden amongst them
hidden in plain sight.

everyone agreed
that I was to blame
I ruined this family
I went and told
even though our secret
was not new or old.

culture and family
are both so beautiful
except for when it comes to this
"*Mija*, God hasn't given me strength.
He won't let me let him go."

and so now I mourn
what our relationship used to be.
I still see you now and then
now much more healed,
brave, and grown
but now when we speak
there is so much left unsaid
because
I have had
enough.

Gracias a Dios
Carmen Benavides-Garb

"Escuchar para aprender y aprender a escuchar, esta historia ocurrió una vez en un pueblo muy remoto donde la gente hablaba una cierta girozoncia (made up word)." This is how my Abuelita Elsita would start all of her stories. Standing at 5 ft tall she commanded any room she entered. She had a scar going from her hairline to through her eye, due to a major car accident years ago. She had short gray hair and wore colorful sweaters. She had 4 kids and grew up in the countryside. She never went to high school and loved playing "Escoba" (naipe, card game). She helped teach me how to make empanadas, Chile's national dish. She was a devout Baptist woman. As a kid it would amaze me that she would just like sitting for hours reading the bible again and again. I couldn't understand how someone could believe in something so fiercely that they cannot see. She could recite bible verses off the top of her head, her own bible was filled with annotations, highlighted sections, underlined in blue ink. She would always tell me and my brothers' folk stories as if she was performing in front of an audience of thousands. I always think she was meant for the stage, she had a beautiful singing voice, maybe if life didn't deal her the cards it did, she would've been a singer. She had a traditional view on marriage and gender roles, she is the only person in the world who would tell me I had to prepare myself for a husband, and she was the only person in the world I would not contest when she did. I have a thousand small memories of Abuelita Elista but looking back I didn't know her all too well. I wonder what she was like at my age. What her dreams were, her hopes, did she ever question the God she loved so dear? Abuelita was the matriarch in my family tree, and she brought light wherever she went. I'd like to remember her this way.

Abuelita Elsita had Alzheimer's and it got increasingly worse as she got older. She didn't know who I was during her final years, and it was such a conflicting feeling. I was angry that she didn't know who I was, after she had been such a big part of my life, how could I be forgotten so easily. I wasn't mad at her, because I know she wasn't to blame, there was no one to blame in fact, which made it even more infuriating. But throughout the worst of her Alzheimer's, she always remembered her religion. Read her bible. Preached about God. I have never believed in God in a traditional sense, or found much use in organized religion. But seeing how it got Abuelita through the toughest moments in her life; fleeing her home country, leaving her husband, losing her memory, I feel more connected to religious people. Because at the end of the day for Abuelita, God was hope, regardless of if I thought it was real or not, it helped her and she was able to overcome through faith; how could I ever disregard religion after that? This was one of the biggest lessons she taught me, to see value in religion and to see the positive impacts it had on her.

We knew Abuelita was dying a few weeks before her passing. Her health was slowly declining and she wasn't talking. I was so scared to visit her in her final days, to see her bedridden, to see the most powerful woman I've known in such a vulnerable state almost felt invasive. She had created an image of who she was in my memory, one that didn't match the small frail woman on the cot. She passed away last year, when I was at a math class. We were leaving for Chile that same day to drop my brother off there for his year abroad. We were returning back to the motherland and she was going on; we were all going home. As we said our final goodbyes before our flight, I thought to myself if there is a god Abuelita Elsita is definitely going to be first in line to go through the gates of heaven. She has a spot there; she gave her life to her God. I prayed that day for the first time in years, to a god I didn't believe in, for her sake, that he guide her to heaven. This was one of the only times in my life where I felt peace through God. Abuelita would be so proud, gracias a dios, as she would say.

Gregorio Muniz (x3)
By Gregorio Muniz

Three people
With the same
Name
Each with a
Different
Untold story

I don't know
Much about
GRANDPA
He was a
Bracero.

My dad and
I ARE
Distant
But live together
I know he
Graduated HS
Migrated to California
Met mom
Provided as a
Dad
I still don't
Know
him

I can't wait
For you
To have a
Boy
A wife
A family
Carry on the
Name
How do I
Tell them?

It ends with
Me

Always told me
Who
To be

I found myself
I know
Me
But they don't
I want
A
Husband
Adopt kids
With him, I
Want them
To
Carry the
Name
They want blood
Not my
Happiness

Three people
With the
Same name
Three different
Untold stories
Three Generations
A Grandpa, A Dad, A Son

I am Not Afraid
Karen Zurita

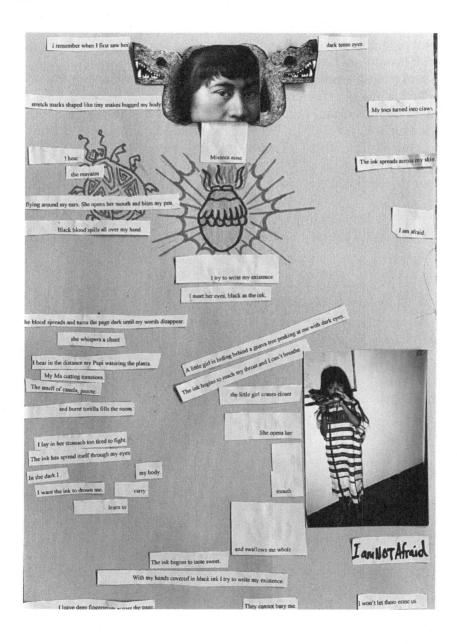

La Mejor Medicina
Marco Antonio Cruz Hernandez

¿Cuál es la acción de sanarse a sí mismo?
¿Será usando medicina como cuando tienes fiebre?
¿O será cuando estás meditando para calmar la mente?
Para mí, sanar es cenar con mi familia.
Hablar de memorias bonitas, chistosas y temas que no nos hacen discutir mucho.
Sanarme es estar a lado de gente que me quiere y que me hace sentir seguro.
Sanar es vivir en la cultura de mi mamá y de los ancestros antes de ella.
No importa lo grave que esté,
La mejor medicina es la familia.

My Debt
Valeria Ruiz

Oh, how much I want to give back
For this once-in-a-lifetime opportunity
The debt I'm in is infinite
For it seems there's no way
To pay it back
But I try, I try
But no matter how much I try
I'll still be in debt
To this life
The life
my mother has given
to me.

Mi deuda

Oh, cuánto quiero devolver
Por esta oportunidad única en la vida
La deuda que tengo es infinita
Parece que no hay manera alguna
De pagarla de vuelta
Pero intento e intento
Pero nunca es suficiente mi esfuerzo
Seguiré en deuda
Con esta vida
Que mi madre me dio.

Naypyidaw
Matt Aung

I am from a land where tyranny lays waste
to the people and culture
Corruption is a part of the history
History rich with spirituality

Ruins of temples past adorn the plains
Grand balloons fill the skies
The ground rusts and decays
And in the mountains lurk
Killers, thieves, and prey

Yet beauty remains; shining through
Like the Jade and Rubies deep below
Crimson like the blood of my family
Yellow like the beating sun
Green like the overgrown foliage
This is where I'm from

Necesidad y Sacrificio: San Ysidro, Su Frontera, y Su Gente
Anitza Monarrez

The San Ysidro Border is the busiest crossing in the country. Composed of rusting sheets of metal that divide thousands of miles of desert, mountain, and water, and armed with a deadly brigade, the U.S. & Mexico Border is one of the most evocative and morally complex structures in this country. But beyond being a monumental structure with a deep and enigmatic history, San Ysidro and its border is the place I call home. Truly a melting pot within the melting pot that is the United States.

Still, I cannot boast or brag because I can't separate the pride from the wearying knowledge and desensitization this place causes its residents. While this country has provided so much for families such as my own, we cannot dismiss the indisputable harm it has caused others. We should not accept or forget the atrocities and indifference of both countries towards immigrants and their families.

I approached this photo series hoping to convey the mundaneness of the border while still capturing its terrifying magnitude and unease. I was looking for a pattern I knew was there. A pattern damped in familiarity. The border is a reminder of human nature; of our adaptability, our resilience, our pride, and our anguish.

I would like to dedicate this series to everyone who has been lost to the deserts, the rivers, to sierras and mountains. To everyone who still waits for their loved ones to come home. And to those who never will. To all the people that have gone missing and to all the people murdered by border patrol. I dedicate this to the people who have no one who looks for or remembers them. To all the kids who never met their grandparents. To the adults who couldn't attend their family member's birthday parties or funerals. For all the kids whose identities are affected by the disconnect. To everyone who doesn't speak their native tongue and to the code switchers. To the multiple generations under one roof that can't communicate. I also dedicate this piece to the thousands of people caged by US authorities. To the hundreds who were hurt during the riots, and to the people who gave birth as they waited to cross.

Interviews

The following have been translated from Spanish. Much of the sentimental weight of these interviews is lost in translation.

Señora Magdalena is a 68-year-old woman from Nayarit. I talked with her while she was getting ready to go back to Mexico. She had multiple woven bags she used as her luggage. She had crossed to visit her son in Bakersfield for Thanksgiving, a holiday she explained was important only because she got to see her son and grandkids. Her son had moved to the United States about ten years ago, he finished school, married and lives comfortably with his wife and two sons.

Are you ready to go back home?

Of course! I'm a little sad about leaving my son and grandkids but I miss my home (mi tierra).

We conversed a little about her town and she reminisced about a time when her husband was alive and her kids still needed to be tucked in at night. There was comfort in those memories. A warmth I did not see in her features when we talked about la frontera. I asked:

What do you feel when you see the border? The fence and the barbed wire?

It's ugly. [laughs] Someone needs to take better care of it. The crossing itself is better but the rest of the fence is not well maintained.

When you cross, do you feel welcomed?

People can be very rude. They're not very patient with people that, like me, don't speak English. I've been visiting for so long I know where to find people like me. We're everywhere, I know where I'm welcomed.

Considering the distance, the separation, and the different culture your family is adopting and growing with, what does the opportunity of crossing mean to you? What does it mean to your family?

I'm very grateful for it. I'm very proud of my son for his struggles. Life in the United States is not easy but it's worth it. I would like to see him more often, and he's offered to get me papers but I don't want to move here. I know my son knows who he is and is proud of where he comes from. He knows he'll always have a home in Nayarit.

We talked about the immigrant experience for a moment and then I walked her to the gate. I asked to take her picture and she flusteredly declined. She felt underdressed.

I walked around and took more pictures of my surroundings. By the time I walked back to where I met Magdalena, it was night time. I saw a group of men huddled together, waiting for a bus. They had small carry-on bags and wore many layers of clothing. I asked a gentle faced man where they were going, he told me they were here to work. I walked down the group and spotted a man that looked much younger than the rest. I approached him.

Manuel is a 26 years old man from Tijuana. He is in the United States on a temporary work visa. His destination is Sacramento. I asked him if this was his first time coming to work, he said no. He had been 23 when he started. He is a father of two girls, ages 5 and 3. They stay in Mexico with his wife. I asked him the same questions I asked Magdalena:

What do you feel when you see the border? The fence and barbed wire?

Lots of things. It's very dirty and unkempt on both sides. But I didn't come here to live in luxury. I come in, make my money, and get out. Trapped by the fence, so far from my family, and looked down upon by the locals make me feel excluded. All that goes away when I get to Sacramento or Alaska, wherever I go to work next. I've been with this group a couple years now. They're like my little family now. My little piece of home.

When you cross, do you feel welcomed?

No. Well, it depends. Border patrol is very rude to people like me. They look at you like you're dirty. Like you are lesser to them. But beyond that I think so. We travel in groups and house together during the season. I have friends here.

What does the opportunity of crossing mean to you? What does it mean to your family?

It's a great opportunity. I feel very blessed to have health and strength to work. It's a break from my routine. Thanks to this money my family lives well. We have a roof over our heads, food on the table. Vacation trips and good birthday parties. In those three months I miss my girls a lot but I work hard so their lives are better than mine.

We talked about he told me a little more about his daughters and wife. He had to drop out of school to provide for his pregnant wife. He works in construction mostly, but he takes odd jobs here and there. He didn't work the salmon run earlier this year because one of his daughters had been sick so he's going to Sacramento to work the field instead. His wife continues to go to school. She's studying to be an industrial engineer. He would like to go back to school one day. He wants to become an engineer too. I asked to take a picture of him, he declined jokingly saying his wife might get jealous.

Coming to this country can be a big adjustment for people. Simply visiting can feel alienating and disorienting. As hard as others may try to erase our roots, we cannot forget who we are and where we come from. This country is its people, and its people are beautiful and diverse.

The Healing Words of Nature
Sky Kili

Since I was a baby,
I was born into a storm
But before I hit the open air
I was safe and I was warm

Inside, mi casa was filled with sound
Yelling, Screaming, all so loud
Outside, in the autumn breeze
River wrapping 'round my knees
Ancient melodies of feathered friends
Reminding me of where I belong

In the roots of the willow
I am safe and warm
Deep in her bosom
I withstand all storms

Una Vida Sin Mamá y Hermanos
Luis Eduardo Rodriguez

Sí, es muy difícil tratar de vivir sin tu madre, sin ustedes hermanos. Cada día me levanto pensando en que algún día ustedes estarán conmigo, porque no pararé de esforzarme hasta que ustedes estén a mi lado. He llorado y sufrido, pero yo sé que todo tiene su recompensa. Tú me enseñaste los nobles valores de la vida mamá y por eso estoy muy agradecido. Esos "pórtate bien mijo," "échale ganas a la escuela," y "no hagas vagancias" los llevo en el corazón. He intentado jugar fútbol, baseball, ir al gym para poderme distraer un poco, aún así llego a casa y me pongo a pensar en lo cuanto que los extraño deseando que puedan estar a mi lado.

Los quiero mucho.

Luis

Where Am I From?
By Kimberli Pacheco

I am from Family pictures. From maquinas,
Tortilleras. I am from the Joyous household.
Funny moments, juguetes that are all around.
I am from lirios, that bloom during the summer.
From Family gatherings and Loteria games.
From Catalina and Ruby.
I´m from the family cooking and chisme.
From meaningful conversations con mi Tía,
Sunday church and videogames with my cousin and
Finally, I am from a one-way city though my blood runs through
Oaxaca, Mexico
and from those Sunny days where we spent time at the river.

Unlearn
Georgina Cerda Salvarrey

Since I was a child, I was filled with stereotypes, with concepts, with self-hatred. Hating myself was the motto, this world told me: you are not thin enough, you are not good enough, nobody will love you if you are not pretty, beauty hurts.. Unlearning is a term that touches everyone, but mainly women. What men learn is that their position within this social hierarchy is higher, and it is true, this position benefits them so much that in some way, on many occasions, it makes them immune to social, cultural and even legal justice.

I had to **Unlearn** fear, turn inside me and see what I was full of and why I was full of exactly those things. **Unlearning** is a process that never ends, little by little I am doing it, and at the same time I wonder **why** I have to unlearn this, why remove it, and why was it inoculated from the beginning. **Unlearn** hatred and fear of what is different, that there is no right way to live life, that I am not always right and that to be right is NOT what matters. **Unlearn** that my judgment is NOT free of bias or discrimination that my privileges give me, **unlearn** that I do not have to be my worst enemy and that I do NOT have to make merits to be deserving.

Understand that I am not alone, and **learn** that the context in which I am allows me to see things from another perspective, a context that I chose precisely because of the pain that I have experienced in my life, the same pain that brings me closer to some of my passions and that thanks to this: I unlearn. In this context, my feminism, is where I mirror myself and echo my stories with the stories of other women. **Unlearn** that my VALUE is NOT in the hands of someone else, and learn that my value is inherent to my essence, and to what I have worked for and lived in my life. Unlearn that I do not ONLY have myself, but that I HAVE MYSELF. There is so much to unlearn yet.

Desaprender
Georgina Cerda Salvarrey

Desde niña fui llenada de estereotipos, de conceptos, de odio a mí misma. Odiarme a mí misma era la consigna, este mundo me decía: no eres lo suficientemente delgada, no eres lo suficientemente buena, nadie te va a querer si no eres bonita, la belleza duele, etc.. Desaprender es un término que nos toca a todos, pero principalmente a las mujeres. Lo que aprenden los hombres es que su puesto dentro de esta jerarquía social es más alto, y es cierto, este puesto los beneficia tanto que de alguna manera, en muchas ocasiones, los hace inmunes a algunas adversidades e impunes a la justicia social, cultural y hasta legal.

Desaprender el miedo, voltear hacia dentro y ver de que estaba llena y porqué estaba llena de lo que estaba llena. Desaprender es un proceso que no termina nunca, poco a poco lo voy haciendo, y a la vez que me pregunto porqué lo tengo que desaprender, porqué extirparlo, y porqué se me inoculó desde un principio. Desaprender el odio y el miedo a lo diferente, que no hay forma correcta de vivir la vida, que no siempre se tiene razón y que eso NO es lo importante. Desaprender que mi juicio NO está libre de sesgos o discriminaciones que me otorgan mis privilegios, desaprender que no tengo que ser un verdugo conmigo misma y que NO tengo que hacer méritos para ser merecedora.

Entender que no estoy sola, y aprender que el contexto en el que estoy me permite ver las cosas desde otra perspectiva, un contexto que yo elegí precisamente por el dolor que he experimentado en mi vida, el mismo que me acerca a algunas de mis pasiones y que gracias a esto: desaprendo. Es ahí, en el contexto de mi feminismo donde me espejeo y hago eco de mis historias con las historias de otras morras. Desaprender que mi valía NO está en manos de alguien más, y aprender que mi valor es inherente a mi esencia, lo que he trabajado y vivido en mi vida. Desaprender que no SÓLO me tengo a mi misma, sino que me TENGO A MI MISMA. Hay tanto que desaprender aún.

Chapter 2
Invierno : Winter

Dejar Todo Sin Dejar Nada
Andrea Itzel Velazco Quiroz

Dejar mi vida, dejar mi alma, eso es lo que sentí mientras más lejos estaba.
Sentirme alejada, sentirme tan extraña, entre otro idioma y otras paradas.
Es tan extraño no saber qué hacer, cuando yo antes lo tenía todo calculado.
En realidad, no me arrepiento, pero de verdad cuánto extraño.
Te extraño mamá, te extraño hermano,
por favor no lo olviden porque saben en realidad cuánto los amo.
Mami no estoy sola ahora, me acompaña mi hermana y mi hermano en mis pasos.
Mamá no estás tú realmente ahorita a mi lado, pero créeme que daría todo porque estuvieras a nuestro lado,
con mi hermana, mis hermanos, conmigo.
Pero no, maldita frontera, ¿por qué nos separas?, ¿por qué nos alejas?, frontera no existas!
Lo que tuve que dejar, de las personas que me tuve que alejar, y a lo que me tuve que acostumbrar a no tener más, todo porque tú estás a la mitad de nuestro lugar.
Pero hay algo que siempre pienso y pienso, en realidad ellos ahí están, mi vida ahí está, todo lo que forma y formó parte de mi vida ahí está, solo cambié de lugar para aún poder crear cosas nuevas y progresar.
Sufrí, claro que sufrí, pero de algo estoy segura: el cambio es para seguir.
Claro que extraño, claro que anhelo volver otra vez, a esa tierra en la que tanto experimenté.
Y de algo estoy segura, mi mamá pronto estará acá.
Porque es difícil experimentar sin tenerla a ella para que me pueda aconsejar, y para eso está mi hermana lo sé, me ha apoyado mucho, pero seamos sinceros varios necesitamos a nuestra mamá.

Luna Sleeping
Nayali Abarca

Dejar a Mis Padres
Luis Camacho Garcia

Dejar a mis padres, decirlo es tan fácil pero cada kilómetro que me alejaba de ellos dolía más y más. No suelo ser alguien que comparta sus sentimientos, así que nunca digo esto. Haber estado con ellos siempre y luego, en un solo momento, tomar la decisión de alejarme de casa para irme a otro país ha sido algo muy duro. Estar solo, tener que lidiar con todos mis problemas, trabajar, estudiar y tomar responsabilidades de adulto, siendo que antes siempre tenía el apoyo de mis padres. Tener que aguantar ese sentimiento de soledad a diario, las ganas de verlos, hablar con ellos sobre mis problemas. Siempre que estoy hablando con ellos por teléfono, solo tengo que decir que todo está bien para que mamá no llore. Perdón mamá, perdón papá. Ahora ya entiendo porque eran sus regaños o castigos, pero creo que me di cuenta de las consecuencias muy tarde. Si tan solo hubiera seguido todos esos consejos, las cosas hubieran salido mejor. Pero creo que todos estos golpes han sido solo enseñanza para dejar la actitud de niño e intentar convertirme en un hombre. Ahora solo espero cumplir todos esos sueños que le conté a mamá y que se pueda dar cuenta que su niño lo logró.

Basil & Rose
Covin Sigala

Descubriendo
Joahnna Tool

A veces me hace triste pensar en todos los años que trate de ser algui-
en que no era; especialmente en ese lugar.
Ese lugar
lleno de personas que no se ven como yo;
los que siempre me miraban y decidían quién era
mucho más antes de que yo pudiera descubrirme a mí misma.

En ese lugar me hicieron sentir
que la lengua que hablaba,
la ropa con que vestía, y
como me miraba
eran cosas que tenía que
suprimir, borrar y destruir.

Ahora sé
que lo único que necesitaba
era escapar de
ese lugar.

Recientemente me preguntaron si llamo
ese lugar mi hogar y
si estaba orgullosa del lugar en que crecí
mi respuesta a sus preguntas fue-
¡NO!

En estos últimos años he descubierto más claro que nunca de lo que si
me trae orgullo.

Estoy orgullosa
de ser Mexicana y Guatemalteca,
de mis ancestros
de mis antepasados,
de la lengua que hablo.

¡Estoy descubriendo quien soy por mí misma y no por cómo me
definen los demás!

How Riverside County Celebrates Historical Indigenous Oppression
Logan Roselli

I grew up in Riverside County in Southern California. I say Riverside County because I really grew up in a multitude of cities within the county. I moved around within the same general area from the edge of Lake Elsinore, to Corona, to Norco, and then to Riverside. Though all of these cities have their own unique circumstances, the general themes more or less stay the same. Though I didn't always live in Riverside, Riverside was always a big part of my life. Both of my parents have worked in Riverside as long as I've been alive and I always visited the shops, went out with my friends, attended events and worked in Riverside. My movement throughout the county and my life in a solidly middle-class family has allowed me to experience the beauty and the pain that is present in all parts of the Inland Empire. The issues most often discussed are a lack of water, drug abuse, and homelessness. Those that are less talked about, but still present to those looking, are gang violence, gentrification, the celebration of colonization, and indigenous erasure. The Inland Empire does not face one of these challenges more than any of the others, they are simply all consequences and ailments of each other. However, all of their roots can be traced back to colonization and the continued celebration of genocide.

The colonization of Riverside began when Spanish explorers moved up from Mexico and until they found the Santa Ana River. The tribes native to this land are the Cahuilla, Juaneño, Gabrieleno, and Luiseño. The most prominent of all these tribes were the Luiseño and many live in the area to this day. The Inland Empire is drier today than it has ever been, but that doesn't mean that it was ever flowing with water either. The Santa Ana River was vital for the survival of all who lived in the land, providing both food and water. The Spanish long ago took control of the river, but after the Mexican-American war, the Riverside Water Company took control and has faced numerous related lawsuits throughout its history. An extensive photo essay written by John W. Lantz documents that "The [Riverside Water Company] and its parent companies were involved in over twenty-five lawsuits involving liability, property, and water rights" (2004). Clearly, this is indicative of a lack of alignment between public interest and those of the company.

The Santa Ana River still runs through Riverside County and Orange County straight out to the ocean. It also still provides a great deal of the water utilized by those living in the local areas. However, it is more known for providing recreational opportunities even though it is seldom used for such purposes. Growing up, my friends and I were some of the few that frequently enjoyed the benefits of the river. In fact, I have seen only twenty or so people in the areas of the river that are accessible from the City of Corona and I used to visit the area multiple times a week. In addition to the Santa Ana River, the Cleveland National Forest is also a part of the area where I grew up. Though it is considered a national forest, the parts that I know do not resemble a forest at all and very few plants are higher than my shoulder. Still, it is a beautiful and vast place to explore and identify native flora and fauna. It is one of the few places in the area that is not directly touched by the colonization of the land, though it can still be seen indirectly through its dryness and the presence of invasive species. These access points to nature were my primary source of entertainment growing up and places of extreme comfort when I needed it most.

In town, I often visited the Tyler Mall because, although I didn't have much money to spend until I was older and began working, my friends and I could go and pretend like we might buy things and feel independent. I smile to myself today when I visit the place and see kids doing the same thing. The day after I turned 16, I got my license and began driving my grandpa's old 2007 Honda Pilot with nearly 300,000 thousand miles on it. In a car-centric place like Southern California, being able to drive opens up an entirely new world of possibilities. I began to visit the Van Buren Drive-In, go to downtown Riverside much more frequently, and visit natural places like Mount Roubidoux and the California Citrus State Historical Park. Despite its age and its constant issues, I loved my car because it could fit up to eight people meaning that all my friends could fit in it when going places. Traffic in Southern California is absolutely terrible and I spent a lot of time in my car, so much so, that I would consider my car itself a space. To me, my car meant freedom and a private space where I could be temporarily away from the distractions of life. Car culture is a big deal in the Inland Empire and many people use their cars as a show of status. Many of my friends participated in street races and there are car shows or meet-ups almost every weekend.

Riverside, just as many cities, has a history of erasing the past of its native populations. If one were to search online for "things to do in Riverside," some of the top results are the Mission Inn and Mount Roubidoux. Two places that I found comfort in visiting growing up. Yet, despite the importance of these landmarks to today's community, they represent a history of oppression and a continued celebration of colonization. The Mission Inn was never a real Spanish Mission. It was constructed over a hundred years ago to look like a Spanish Mission for the purpose of attracting tourists who were interested in seeing the real missions of California. Encouraging tourists to stay at a luxurious place, not indicative at all of how real Native Americans were forced to live is of course problematic, but the owners also established a working relationship with the Sherman Institute, a federal Native American boarding school. Those traveling to the city of Riverside were promised that they would see "real live Indians" at the Sherman Institute (Whalen 2013). In fact, the Sherman Institute was originally based in L.A. County, but the owner of the Mission Inn convinced officials to move it to Riverside because he thought it would boost tourism and enthusiasm for his hotel (Rice 2017). Of course, things have improved over time, but the Mission Inn still is an exhibition of oppression. Racism can take up a physical space, and this often happens through the design of buildings (Perez 2022). The Mission Inn is designed to look like a mission, but it is also intended to contain many more people than a real mission would have been. Consequently, the property is surrounded by tall walls and behind those tall walls are even taller buildings. Furthermore, the hotel is a luxury hotel and prices for a room designed for two adults in December 2022 do not fall below $329 per night. The combination of extremely high prices and unwelcoming architecture create a tone that is clearly not inviting members of the community, especially not those that the hotel and its owners have historically disenfranchised.

Mount Roubidoux is the highest reachable physical location anywhere in downtown. It is a popular spot for locals and visitors alike to exercise and enjoy the day. It has a few trails, varying in difficulty, but all the trails feature fragments of buildings left behind from Spanish colonizers. At the peak of the mountain, where all the trails end up, a huge cross is planted, towering over any who come to visit it. The cross, as well as other landmarks, are dedicated to Father Junipero Serra, one of the most infamous colonizers in California's history. Once again, spatial-culture politics come into play. The towering of the monument and its point as the highest peak in the nearby area represent and are a reminder of the oppression that was once readily apparent, and the oppression that silently perseveres today.

Recognition of the continued impacts of colonization are hard to find in Riverside. However, the community is beginning to reclaim the space through the multitude of local museums that are willing to celebrate the indigenous culture and recognize the impacts of the various local players. One of these museums is the Riverside Art Museum. Filled with a collection of various pieces, the museum constantly changes its exhibits and features local artists and items of historical significance. I remember around the winter holidays many years ago I visited the museum to see the exhibit on concert posters, but in addition to the exhibit I came to see, I also discovered a temporary exhibit celebrating historical Indigenous religion. I remember very clearly a small sculpture of a wind god. At the time, I was very interested in ancient European religions and this was the first time I had ever seen an Indigenous god represented. The Riverside Art Museum has opened this year a separate museum, called The Cheech. The Cheech is managed by the Riverside Art Museum but contained in its own building and functions somewhat independently of the general museum. The Cheech was founded by Cheech Marin of Cheech and Chong and is dedicated to celebrating Indigenous and Chicano art. The museum has been in progress for several years and had numerous fundraisers within the community to help fund the project. Every event received an outpouring of support and the community has rallied around the museum. The new museum is so beloved that I have not been able to visit it beyond the front doors because every time I have tried, the building has reached capacity and cannot allow any more visitors.

Despite the dark and often forgotten history of Riverside, it is a community of diversity and of growth. The creation of spaces for the diverse community like The Cheech are strong indicators of progress toward a more equitable future. Cities in Riverside County that are considered the worst places to live are beginning to increase the number of community events, and those events are often focused on celebrating the diverse people present in the towns. Access to nature, public places designed for education, and rich culture are all proven to increase the quality of life in a city and all of these qualities are present in the city of Riverside. Present, just often forgotten. By acknowledging the Indigenous cultures expelled from our home, we are provided with the opportunity to take action and to stop choosing to forget.

Works Cited:

Lantz, John W. "California Land, Water, and Law: A History of the Riverside Water Company, 1870 to 1983." *ProQuest*, California State University, Fullerton, 2004.

Perez, Nancy. "[Lecture Slides] ES 107- Section 3 Week 10." California, Arcata.

Rice, Christina. "The Sherman Institute of Riverside, California: A History in Photos." *The Sherman Institute of Riverside, California: A History in Photos*, Los Angeles Public Library, 2017.

Whalen, Kevin. "Finding the Balance." *American Behavioral Scientist*, vol. 58, no. 1, 2013, pp. 124–144.

La Madrugada Amarga
Gerber Campos

Les presentaré una parte de mi vida en Guatemala. Recuerdo que una semana antes de junio, viví los peores días de mi vida a causa de una decisión de muerte. Un sueño, una meta desafiando mi vida a través de un camino angosto, un sueño que pocos logran.

Un viaje hacia un lugar a un mundo existencial que todos nos imaginamos. Hacia un país de riquezas donde la pobreza no existe y donde una persona se puede volver millonaria, pero no. Como dice un dicho "hasta no probar no saber."

Recuerdo dos días antes de partir hacia ese viaje "maravilloso", pasé las noches más alentadoras escuchando el susurro de las aves. Sentí una tristeza oscura en llanto y dolor por pensar en dejar toda mi vida, mi familia, amigos y seres queridos atrás.

El jueves 29 de agosto de 2021 fue el último día que trabajé con mis padres. Recuerdo ese momento como si fuera ayer. Cerré el local, me senté en una esquina donde había una silla y pude sentir una vibración en mi cuerpo que me estremecía, sabiendo que era sensible y con un corazón despistado. Recordé cada momento de felicidad con mis padres y hermanas, comiendo y disfrutando en armonía y gozo y dando gracias a Dios por su ayuda del día a día.

Y sin darme cuenta, en un cerrar y abrir de ojos, el día había finalizado. Me acuerdo de esas horas y momentos que pasaban con una tristeza inimaginable, pero llegó la cena y todos estábamos comiendo pollo horneado, mi comida favorita. Estábamos tan felices disfrutando y viviendo en familia hasta que terminamos de comer. Quien diría que ese momento tan especial se convertiría en un sueño mortal del cual nunca podría despertar.

Llegó la hora de dormir, pero no lo logré. Me ahogaba en llanto de lágrimas sabiendo que a las 4 de la mañana me tocaba irme para siempre de sus vidas sin saber cuándo los volvería a ver.

Le di un abrazo a mis hermanas con mi corazón en mil pedazos. Me acerqué a mi linda madre, ella estaba junto con mi padre. Recuerdo ese momento donde abracé con todo mi ser a mi hermosa madre, la cual daría su vida por mí. Recordé todas sus caricias y regaños. Después miré a mi padre con una mirada sensible y pude ver a través de sus ojos el dolor que sentía. Me arrodillé ante ellos pidiéndoles perdón por todo y su bendición.

Mis padres me abrazaron tan fuerte que pude sentir el amargo dolor que les dejaba en sus vidas. Nunca me había separado de ellos, pero llegó el día y el momento de cambiar mi vida. Llegaron las 4 de la mañana, me levanté del suelo y me alisté. Me puse mi mochila y mis padres me dejaron solo en una parada. Ese fue el último día que miré sus rostros. Ellos me dijeron "cuídate, todo va a salir bien, lucha por tu vida, tú puedes salir adelante, lo vas a lograr y lo dirás enfrente a nosotros algún día."

Se fueron los dos, me dejaron solo con mi mochila. Una gran tristeza me invadía y mi corazón se partía en mil pedazos mientras se iban. Me dieron ganas de salir corriendo hacia ellos, pero no pude, ya había tomado la decisión del "sueño americano, el supuesto país de las maravillas."

Ahora estoy esforzándome en un país donde no sé el idioma y todo es diferente a mi país. Estoy logrando esa meta, esforzándome, sacrificando mis estudios y trabajando a la misma vez. A veces me siento frustrado y enredado en este país. Yo sé que puedo hacerlo, recuerdo cada instante vivido con mi familia y sé que lo lograré porque le hice esa promesa a mi familia. Porque soy un hombre de palabra.

Untitled (Mess No. 1)
Jesse Morales

Juntes (Ode to In Lak'ech)
Marisol Ruiz, Griselda Valdez, Mayra Meza,
and Georgina Cerda Salvarrey

Dedicamos este poema to CA ban on In Lak'ech

Espejos
    Reflejan
        Miradas conocidas
    Sagradas
Transcendentes

Me veo
    En tí
        Estamos juntos
    Respetando
Nuestros caminos

Hombro a hombro
    Hiking through
        Mountain tops
    I see your reflection
In me
    Have I lost myself
        In you?
           Or have I become
              A new version
                Of me?

Mi Recuerdo Inolvidable
Jose Maceda

Cuándo llegué a Estados Unidos tenía 17 años. Cuándo llegué tenía absolutamente nada. Toda mi vida se quedó en México y aquí tendré que empezar de cero. Es un lamento muy desagradable pues dejé mi hogar, mis amigos, mi familia, mi comunidad y mi país. Emigre a Estados Unidos para cumplir mi sueño americano. Pero ahora ví todo lo que se sufre en la frontera: días caminando, cuidando la comida y el agua. Me daba miedo acabarme toda la comida y quedarme sin nada. Ví a mucha gente sufriendo y me sentía mal de no poder ayudarlos, de no poder hacer nada. Los días eran soleados, hacía un calor sofocante pero las noches eran frías y oscuras. Cuando por las madrugadas descansábamos, sentía un cansancio agotador. Me dolían los pies de tanto caminar y hacía un frío que me hacía temblar hasta los huesos. Es algo traumante que nunca voy a olvidar, y que nunca quiero volver a vivir.

Miedo
Griselda Valdez, Mayra Meza, and Gina Cerda Salvarrey

Fear of not being enough
Fills my thoughts
Overwhelms my mind
Fear of failure paralyzes me
And leaves me behind

El miedo se mueve y nos envuelve
Miedo al miedo
A la parálisis
A dejar de luchar y parar
A ser borrada y que mis gritos se pierdan en la nada
A dejar que la injusticia se eleve

Confront the fear
Transforma el miedo
Sacudiéndolo, hablándolo
Looking for my inner peace
Being now and here
Para poder actuar
Y encontrar la paz within me
Because I am enough

Nuestros Pasos En Algo Diferente
Christo Santiago

Dime ¿por qué? por favor ¿por qué me pasó todo eso en mi niñez?

Amá, Apá, díganme ¡¿por qué?! y por favor díganme ¿por qué de niño siempre me comparaban con otros niños que estaban a mi lado? Siempre que me comparaban, sentía que las cosas que yo hacía no eran suficientes. A lo mejor era cierto o a lo mejor no, era difícil saber porque yo era muy pequeño

When I was around four, it was hard to understand what others said. I know I'm not the only one in this world that struggles with learning something. I was only taught one language at that time. It was the same language that we all used to communicate with our families.

De niño, me apuraba mucho aprender el idioma de inglés. No era algo fácil de aprender. Siempre que iba a la escuela no podía tener amigos, ni podía entender el idioma que otros hablaban. Siempre me sacaban de mi clase para estar en otro salón. Todos los días estaba yo solo con una maestra aprendiendo cómo leer y escribir, por muchas horas. Mientras que estaba sentado yo podía ver desde la ventana a los otros niños jugando afuera, mientras que yo estaba con unos libros enfrente de mí. Hasta en la casa me quedaba despierto, estudiando hasta las 9 de la noche, sentado con mi Amá en el sofá.

Al mismo tiempo mi Amá aprendía un poco de inglés conmigo, pero todavía recuerdo cómo me pegaba en la cabeza cuando ella pensaba que yo decía una palabra mal, aunque la hubiera dicho bien.

Tenía una familia, eran como mi familia porque ellos me ayudaron mucho con el inglés. Un día falleció David y fue muy difícil vivir sin él a mi lado. Después de su muerte me daba pena hablar, sentía que había perdido la habilidad de hablar inglés.

Tu hijo Cristo F. Santiago

Ode to the One That Raised Me
Chelsea Rios Gomez

All of my pain is still fresh.
I carry it around everywhere I go.
But my pain isn't my pain.
It's our pain.
This life isn't my life.
It's yours.
Tell me what to do and I'll listen.
Tell me what to wear and I'll change.
Tell me what to eat and I'll make it.
I'll sacrifice everything and anything that makes me whole.
I'll break off my pieces to make you whole.
Yet, I know it won't be enough.
Nothing can make you proud.
You seek to fill your own emptiness vicariously through me.
But I know you do it subconsciously.
How broken do I have to be for you to realize that the issue isn't me?
How broken do I have to be for me to realize that the issue isn't me?
I am left alone to pick up the pieces of what's left of me.
I spent all my life begging you to love me.
I never learned to love myself, even less how to accept someone's help.
We are two broken souls trying to love each other without knowing what love is.
So we love each other brokenly.
And we love each other painfully.
But we love each other wholeheartedly.
That's what makes me, me.
The passion and strength to keep loving.
The passion and strength to keep fighting.
I don't blame you.
You're a reflection of circumstance and I am too.
You taught me resilience. You taught me greatness.
I am strong. I am brave. I am all the great things you are.
I wouldn't be where I am today without you.
So I write an ode to the one who raised me.
Trust me when I say that our pain ends with me.

Mis Placas Tectónicas: La Culpa, La Tristeza y El Coraje
Tim Olson

Después de 18 años todavía existe el dolor y la tristeza enterrados profundamente en mi ser, en mi corazón y en mi alma. A veces suben y salen, provocados por algo, una memoria, una foto, un recuerdo, como un gran terremoto provocado por el movimiento de las placas tectónicas en lo profundo de la tierra. Porque en lo profundo de mi ser hay tres placas tectónicas:

1. La culpa que siento, me siento culpable por la confusión y el dolor que le causamos a nuestros hijos con el divorcio.
2. La tristeza que siento por destruir el sueño de tener una familia.
3. El coraje que siento por todo el tiempo que perdí de estar con mis hijos y que nunca voy a poder recuperar, coraje por todas las veces que mi ex me acusó de no ser un buen padre.

Estos sentimientos están enterrados profundamente en mi ser, bajo tanta presión, que con una sola provocación: ¡BOOM! Hay otro estallido de emociones.

Este verano pasado, me mudé y tuve que revisar todas mis pertenencias. Encontré una canción que yo había escrito sobre el tiempo difícil, justo antes de que tomáramos la decisión de separarnos y divorciarnos. Todos los sentimientos y emociones desde hace 19 años regresaron rápidamente, embistiendo, pegándome, atropellándome, dejándome en un mar de lágrimas que no cesaban de correr. El temblor de emociones fue el más grande que había sentido en toda mi vida. Me tumbó como si se me hubieran caído una caja de ladrillos encima. Pensaba que había lidiado con todas estas emociones a través de los años, pero todavía estaban allí, en lo más profundo de mi ser.

Lo que me sana, lo que me calma, lo que me cura, son mis hijos. Ellos son la prueba verdadera de que todo salió mejor de lo que yo esperaba, a pesar de toda la tristeza, la culpa y el coraje. Ellos son exitosos, felices, rodeados por amor, amistades, familia y todo lo bueno de la vida. Su buena salud, física y mental, su felicidad, sus éxitos, son los medicamentos que me curan las heridas causadas por el divorcio. Me hacen darme cuenta de que la tristeza, la culpa y el coraje nunca vencerán y que triunfará el amor que mis hijos y yo tenemos.

Four-Leafed Clovers
Audriana Peñaloza

Dedicated to my friends

I once heard that finding a good friend was like finding a four-leafed clover.

Very difficult, but worth the time and effort put in to find the little thing.

And you would be very lucky if you did find one.

As a kid, finding a friend was extremely easy.

Sharing your gansitos during lunchtime was all that it took.

Then we grow up.

We grow up and few are very lucky to have their four-leafed clover through the awkward years.

Many are not.

Suddenly, we are adults.

We have responsibilities. We have no time. And we are full of anxiety!

I was alone when I got here.

For a long time.

But I found a group of people I could share my gansitos with.

I guess you can say, I am very lucky to have stumbled upon a small patch of four-leafed clovers.

Yes, it was difficult. Yes, it did take a long time. And yes, it did take a whole lot of effort.

But it was all worth it.

You all have taught me what true friendship is,

And there are not enough words in the world to show how thankful I am.

So, I hope this is enough.

Our People
Dillon Avery Harp

Headlines got me ask'n
what we supposed do?
Our People get'n killed
cause we don't look like you
Repression sent subliminal
if you see thugs and criminals
You should lift ya head up
and catch a better view
Cause,
I see Queens and Kings
Raised up in ravines
Just tryna teach they royal youth
to Rage Against Machines

I was raised up in Texas
Lost my soul to the heat
Some of the things I done seen
Man, you'd probably never believe
Different doorways for people
who look like you and me
Different city
Different streets
Different toilets
Different sinks
Different hopes
Different dreams
We might say the same words
but we mean different things

They tell'n me
Anger ain't the answer
I just gotta turn over the page
But Lowkey
reading them census signatures
signed by blind citizens

Got me feel'n enraged
They keep say'n Abe,
Signed a paper
to abolish the pain
But that just means they
Turned the fields
into a cage
Built with tax dollars paid
By a country

Propped up on the
Backs of Slaves.

They call'n us
Indigo kids now
But I ain't talk'n new age
I'm talk'n bout
Melanin bathed
In blue tints made,
Where our ancestors
slaved.

Our people
felt the first
waves crash

A heartbreaking welcome
to the coasts of a New World
As well as
the last sound heard
on the coasts of their past

Our people
moved their feet
bent down on
hand and knee
to feel the earth
change beneath

Our people
reshaped the sounds
their lips made
and the way
their hair laid
But

Our people
Knew that
When

Our people
Gathered at the
End'a the day

Our people's blood
Would always
Speak the Same

Be Proud and Loud
Sydney Leland

Peace is what we want
A fight is what they'll get

Our anger makes you worried

When we are quiet
 we are not moving

Silence is what they want
Being loud is what they'll get

Change does not happen quietly

People learn by being taught
Society stays the same

We are all taught our place in this world
and how to maintain that place
from the moment we are born

Our place in this world is what we make it

If we don't make our place
somebody will make it for you

A place is what we want
A place is what we will not be silent for.

The Aftermath of Absence
Jordan Lavant and Haley Fedalizo

I am from absent parents and present pain,
From court dates and child support.
I am from Zarcufsky family,
But I bear Lavant that opposes Norris.
I am from the conqueror and the conquered,
Whose strength was revealed?

I am from colorful leaves,
Yet, no colorful people.
The mosquitos bite, and so do their words.
I am from frizzy hair, brushed desperately to stay straight.
Stay straight;
I couldn't do that either.

I am from submissive tendencies,
Shoved to the corner, expected to comply.
I am from ringing headaches and fading scars.
Which themselves come from a broken girl
With no understanding of love.

The Maidu and Miwok People in the Wake of California's "Growth"
Benjamin Cross

Growing up in the foothills of the Sierra Nevada Mountain range of California in Auburn placed me on the edge of some of California's best nature in my (biased) opinion. Less than 15 minutes east from where I lived is the confluence of the North and Middle Fork of the American river, and another 10 minutes south finds you by the South Fork. Equally apparent amongst this natural beauty however were the trappings of human development, reservoirs, dams and old dam constructions, quarries, large multi-acre ranches, and of course sprawling suburbs. From a young age I held much more appreciation for the natural beauty in direct proximity to where I lived as opposed to the bland, uninspired cookie cutter repetition of civilization that my day-to-day life was lived in relation to.

This appreciation for nature, and general disdain for development was instilled in me by my father who'd take me and my siblings on frequent hikes by the rivers and around the Sierra Nevadas. In addition to being somewhat of an amateur geologist and botanist, pointing out and identifying various plants and rock formations, my Dad also had a keen interest in the people who had lived for thousands of years prior to European colonization and settlement in the areas we "explored," notably the Maidu and Miwok people. He'd point out and find traces of their habitation for us as we hiked, like obsidian arrowheads, and grinding stones, man-made bowl like indentations left behind on certain rock formations from the repeated grinding of acorns gathered by the Maidu and Miwok peoples from the Black Oaks that grew in proximity to the stones, into a type of flour that would be used in bread and formed a staple part of these people's diets. However, my particular favorite of these traces left behind were the petroglyphs, or a form of ancient rock art, some of which are estimated to be 15,000 years old. In the areas we hiked, these petroglyphs took on a variety of forms, from more abstract shapes like circles, spirals, wavy lines, to more defined figures like stick people and animals. My imagination would always run wild when we stumbled upon some petroglyphs, ascribing potential meanings or symbolism to what we found, but ultimately resigning to the fact there was no way for me to definitively describe what they meant to those who originally made them (or if they were even made as more than mere doodles). However futile it was for me to attempt to understand the intention placed behind the creation of these petroglyphs by the Miwok and Maidu, the intention and symbolism behind grinding stones and leftover tools like arrowheads did not. Represented by these artifacts was the collective desire to live, shared and practiced by these peoples for millennia. But whereas these traces of the Maidu and Miwok people's historic residence in my area filled me with awe whenever I found them, returning home to "civilization" and driving by the towns and homes indicative of present habitation only made me melancholic.

Thinking about why modern examples of human society made me feel such indefinable loss, whereas evidence of Maidu and Miwok society in nature filled me with reverence and hope, I think this difference in feeling comes down to the ways of knowing and approaching the world represented by these respective societies. Evidence of indige-nous peoples' life like bedrock mortars and petroglyphs, show a people who live in a deeply intimate and reciprocal way to the land that con-stitutes their territory, opting for a more dispersed low-impact lifestyle with emphasis placed on understanding/respecting the various forces (themselves included) constituting and maintaining the local ecology, viewing themselves as one strand in a wider web of life. Evidence of modern human life like towns and cities represents a departure from a more environmentally centered epistemology, to one that is anthropo-centric, placing humans as something distinctly separate from nature. In such epistemology humans are at the center, man controls nature not vice-versa, and our very existence/well-being is predicated on the exploitation and absence of nature. Every shopping center as an absence of sprawling meadow, every neighborhood as an absence of forest, every open pit mine as an absence of a mountain, every inch of road and human civilization as an absence of nature existing un-fettered. Even more sickening, modern human life represented in the absence of nature is predicated upon the genocide and extinction of anyone with opposing beliefs, including indigenous peoples around the world resisting subjugation by the nation state.

This sense of loss incurred in me by the existence of most modern development comes from recognition of the incalculable and widespread social damage associated with their colonial legacies. The fact that these cities are currently active and remain inhabited while much of the same and surrounding areas are no longer inhabited by indigenous peoples, who are denied this same right as they're relegated to areas with little or no access to nature and systematically wiped out, speaks to much greater depths of injustice. Moreover, the ongoing colonial legacy of development in California is heavily steeped in environmental injustice, with negative effects as a result "...widespread ecologically harmful practices..." primarily felt by marginalized indigenous peoples and people of color (Pellow and Vazin 2019). In addition to toxic waste disposal sites and air polluting industries being zoned in much greater number by brown communities as opposed to white ones, environmental injustice also manifests in the level of access one has to nature, with in particular communities of color and low-income communities on average lacking safe nearby outdoor spaces for recreation as opposed to majority white communities (Coleman 2022). A concept that further helped frame my thoughts was Jose Esteban Muñoz's idea of the brown commons. This refers to a commons of people, places, things, feelings who are made a commons by their shared experiences of exploitation and struggle under racial capitalism and at collective attempts at imagining alternatives to this exploitative dynamic (Muñoz 2020). The petroglyphs, artifacts and other traces left behind by indigenous peoples in California and the United States can be seen as a representation of this brown commons, offering insights into the ways in which indigenous peoples lived in relation to the natural world, as well as breaking down the supposed divide between land and body through the history embodied in these traces. Laura Aguilar's nature self-portrait photography contributes to this brown commons in that it centers and catalogues brown bodies as being included in natural settings (Venegas 2017), in much the same way that petroglyphs and other rock art left behind by indigenous peoples offers a kind of record of their relation and intimacy with nature.

What will remain of the cities we've built in a millennium? What will they tell about us? Will the blood baked into the bricks condemn us in the eyes of historians? If nothing else, our cities will stand testament to our denial and attempted domination of nature, just as petroglyphs stand testament to our existence under the belief we are a part of nature.

Works Cited:

Coleman, Madia, et al. "The Nature Gap." *Center for American Progress.* (2022).

Muñoz, José Esteban. "Brown Commons" in Chambers-Letson and Nyong'o (eds.), *The Sense of Brown* (2020). Duke University Press. **pp.1-7.**

Pellow, David and Vazin, Jasmine. "The Intersection of Race, Immigration Status, and Environmental Justice." *Sustainability* 11.14 (2019): 3942.

Venegas, Sybil. "Take Me to the River: The Photography of Laura Aguilar" in Epstein, Rebecca (ed.), *Laura Aguilar: Show and Tell* (2017). UCLA Chicano Studies Research Center Press.

Walnuts
Anonymous

The Places We're From
Nico Chorny and Matt Aung

Leaving our nationality
To find a better home
Forming a new personality
Navigating the new I've been shown

Mind fortified by two tongues
Language barriers glorified since I was young,
"¿De dónde eres?" "Where ya from?"
"I don't know, I've always been on the run"

From the East to the West
From the North to the South
Two different people, two different mounds
Searching for identity yet to be found

From the North to the South
From the South to the North
Crossing cultures, determining our worth
These are the places from which we are from

Una Vida Sin Mi Mamá en Otro País
Miriam Rodriguez

Hace casi 4 años que me vine a Estados Unidos porque mi papá quería una vida mejor para mí. Es triste no poder estar con mi mamá porque compartí con ella casi 13 años de mi vida. Ha sido muy doloroso venir a otro país sin ella, sin sus cariños, sin sus abrazos. No tenerla conmigo es muy triste, a veces lloro porque la extraño mucho. Hay veces que necesito un abrazo de ella, sobre todo cuando estoy estresada por la escuela. Necesito sus consejos, como cuando me decía que yo podía. Necesito sentir que ella sí me quiere, porque tengo la sospecha de que mi papá no.

Cuando viví con mi papá, por poco menos de 4 meses, sentí que yo no le importaba. Ahora nomás me habla para preguntarme por mis calificaciones y si están mal nomás me regaña. ¿Qué acaso no quieres saber más de mí?

Pero hay personas que están conmigo: mi tía, mi prima, mis amigas y hablo con mi mamá para contarle de mis días. Paso tiempo con ellas para distraerme y olvidarme de mis problemas. Ellas me levantan, ellas son mi luz que me ilumina. Quiero que ellas estén conmigo toda la vida.

Chapter 3
Primavera : Spring

Somos Músicos
Davis Boone y Mayra Meza

I am from sheet music,
From Vivaldi and Paganini.
I am from the past and future,
Old, remodeled, crushing and baying.

I am from a chancla throwing mother.
From Pinesol and Fabuloso on Sunday mornings.
I am from the two-set house of Shenanigans,
Laughing, joking, playing music at full blast.

I am from el jardín,
Full of life and diversity.
I am from the Pitaya,
Full of thorns to protect but sweet to the taste.

I'm from tents and tenacity.
From Jeff and Paige.
I'm from pozole and tamales.
From Marcelina y Abel Meza.

I'm from borrachos and anger,
From a culture of oppressed people, warriors and mystics.
I'm from the loud laughter and strict discipline,
From "Do it yourself" and "Figure it out".

I'm from Christian faith and better lives
I'm from los isles de Acores, America, Russia, Ireland,
Peixe com creme, camping.

I'm from the minority in all places I go.
I'm from East LA, Puebla and Oaxaca,
Caldo de Pollo, Calabazitas

We are from countless hours of practice.

Agradecida
Kimberlyn Moreno

Yo estoy agradecida por tener la vida que tengo. Growing up, I never really saw my parents struggle, as compared to my brothers. My mom didn't really suffer like my dad did. When my dad was a little kid, he didn't really have much. He would always tell me, he would make toys out of sticks, mud, and bottle caps to make a car or some sort of toy. He started working at a very young age to provide for his family. He was the only man in the house and had to step it up, for his sisters and mother. I never really paid close attention to this. He always has a smile no matter how hard life was for him. That's the thing about my dad. He's a very hard-working man and I look up to that. This taught me to always have a positive mindset. No matter how hard life gets for you, always keep pushing, and good things will happen to you, it's just a matter of time.

A Testimony Denouncing Religion
Kena Arnold-Malufau

My mom is Japanese, and was adopted by a white family. My birth
dad is Mexican.
My adoptive dad is Samoan.
At 18 years old my mom was kicked out of a high school for carrying
me.
At 18 years old my birth dad dropped out of high school, he was
angry with me.
At 18 years old I am the first in my family to go to college.
Now, I am 19 years old and am about to successfully complete a se-
mester of college debt free.
The first time my father abandoned me I was a newborn and he was a
teenager in denial.
He came back when I was two years old.
The last time my father abandoned me I was 13 years old and he was
just as angry as he was when he dropped out of high school. I told
him I was gay. He is Christian.
I used to wonder if he would have still loved me if he wasn't Chris-
tian.
I do not know who I am because I do not know where I come from
My testimony denounces the reason I do not know where I come
from...
Religion burnt that bridge.
a prison pretending to be a home.
Arms open wide, you think they're welcoming but they suffocate you
in obedience to outdated rules that keep you in cages.
I would still talk to my family if religion didn't divide us and our
values, and my family is a key to open the door to know where I come
from.
My life is made up of fragments of 'could have beens':
• I could have spoken Spanish
• I could be in Japan
• I could have not been gay

I *would* be speaking Spanish if I was not gay
If she and I were friends instead of lovers, I would still speak to my

birth father
Who kicked me out at 13
I now know that he was also a prison pretending to be a home.
Trained to never think critically only critique and judge
I denounce a bible that condones homophobia
I denounce a people so wrapped up in their fear that they hide behind a god
Who may or may not have written a book that needs an up-to-date translation.
I denounce a religion that promotes separation.
My family held the torches and pitchforks but pastors taught them how to wield such weapons
I denounce a religion that pretends to be rooted in love,
I denounce a religion that calls poison salvation and spoon feeds it to people to teach them how to hate.

Mejillas Rosadas
Kathryn Lozano

Cambios en 1...2 por 3
Anayka Flores Olguin

Soy de Perú, es el lugar donde nací, pero mi vida cambió en el 2010 cuando tuvimos que viajar mi mamá y yo a los Estados Unidos. Teniendo que dejar a mi papa en Perú y empezar una nueva etapa de mi vida sin él. Yo siempre recordaba los momentos bonitos que pasábamos con mi papá, con sus cariños y bromas también. Me acordaba cuando él siempre me recogía de mi kinder, cuándo estudiaba en Perú. Ahora cada año viajamos para visitarlo y pasar lindos momentos con él, pero cada retorno es cada vez más triste porque sé que no lo volveré a ver por un buen tiempo. Empecé el año escolar con nuevas caras, nuevas cosas y un idioma que no entendía. Fueron unos años difíciles. Todo se me hacía difícil, aún con las ayudas que me daban en la escuela, pues tuve que aprender un idioma nuevo, lo cual no fue fácil. Tuve la ayuda de algunos estudiantes que también hablaban español. Ellos siempre estaban conmigo, así como una profesora que me ayudaba con los trabajos de la escuela. Llegó otro año escolar pero ese año fue aún más difícil, ya que me pedían saber más inglés y escribirlo mejor. Ese año escolar me empezaron a ayudar más, tenía un tutor que me ayudaba en los salones, todo fue difícil pero me miro ahora y digo: lo logré!

La Pantalla
Angel Martinez Toribio

Mi mamá trabajando en CNA y papá trabajando en la construcción o con los carros. A veces papá buscaba trabajo en su computadora e iba a arreglar otras cosas además de carros.

El primer recuerdo que tengo de cuando yo era niño, es estar de pequeño buscando moneditas en cada rincón de la casa para dárselas a mi papá.

Después, cada día siguiente sentía lo mismo. Es triste que me sintiera así. Para mí, eso significó que realmente mi papá no estaba mucho ahí. Solo era una madre luchando contra el mundo para darle de comer a sus hijos. Ella tampoco pasaba mucho tiempo con nosotros. Así que, para no desaparecer de nuestras vidas, o al menos es lo que yo pienso, mi pá nos dio un teléfono para estar en contacto y entretenernos también.

Así crecí con el teléfono, siempre mirando una pantalla.

Luego nos trajo un Xbox con controles y juegos, con una colección de juegos de cartas.

Aunque me gustaban los videojuegos, sabía que la montaña de juegos era peligrosa. Cómo también me gustaba correr y moverme, jugaba en el afterschool program donde aprendí a disfrutar de los juegos de basketball. Competir por algo. Cuándo nos mudamos de casa, perdí las ganas de jugar y sentí que todo lo que había hecho no tenía sentido si me volvería a mudar de nuevo.

Ahora, ya puedo escribir un poquito de mi historia, pero mi problema es: ¿cómo quiero escribir mi futuro?

Locked
Yami E.P.M.

Nunca he podido salir mucho,
es raro.
Me invitan amigos,
me invitan amigas
pero yo no puedo ir.

Mis estrictos padres me dicen:
"No puedes ir porque con una sola vez que salgas, se va a volver una
costumbre."
o me dicen: "
Ahorita tú no me entiendes pero cuando tengas tus hijos, me en-
tenderás."

Yo claro,
no puedo hacer nada
pero obedecerlos.
Esto me da coraje,
enojo e impotencia.

Yo,
todavía pido permiso
esperando por un sí,
sabiendo que será un no.
Pidiendo permiso
me gano
being lectured por horas.

"Má, pá, por favor déjenme salir por un ratito, solo será un ratito,
para distraer la mente." Estoy cansada, of being locked. Estoy cansada
estando en casa todo el tiempo, escuchándolos discutir por las más
tontas razones. Prometo que me portaré bien y que no perderé su
confianza en mí.
I pinky promise!

Body is Soil, Hair is Flower
Minerva Torres

My Garden
By Mia Rose Rios

Coming from such an isolated studio space
Individuals started to sprout into my life.
They were becoming someone important to me,
Reminding me that I belong here with the trees;
Showing me how much growth I have made.
They introduced me to other kind souls.
People who would show me just as much care.

They push me outside my box and bring out a voice,
A voice that can learn to let go of their fears.
I giggle and smile to all the crappy jokes
While we hold each other accountable.
The boring things start to become less hard
And I begin to bloom.

When people walk into the room I stand up tall
Pulling my shoulders back, puffing out my chest.
My silence comforts me in my own space.
But my shyness comes off kind
And I'm told by them that
When I open your mouth,
I always have something meaningful to say.

I'm still afraid and hold back my tongue.
But when I look at all the beautiful growth in my garden,
The plants and people remind me of who I am
And what I'm capable of.
They are my strong roots.

My Mother the Spider
Hunter Circe

"Here is the earth that we have created. It has shape and substance, direction and time, a beginning and an end. But there is no life upon it. We see no joyful movement. We hear no joyful sound. What is life without sound and movement? So you have been given the power to help us create this life. You have been given the knowledge, the wisdom, and the love to bless all the beings you create. That is why you are here."

-The Spider Woman and the Twins, A Hopi Legend

It is not uncommon when concerning the Earth that one envisions a mother. A womb of bountiful life in an ever expanding sea of darkness, pocked with burning bulbs of white hot gas, where cataclysmic clasts of rock and ice loom and solar flares streak and hiss across everlasting night. Despite all that whirls around her, shrouded in darkness, there she sits as an orb of garden suspended in the ether, her children clinging to her. In the solace of her embrace, her children are permitted to create their own life. When I think of the Earth I think of my mother. I think of how her flesh and bones have broken to make mine. I think of how fiercely we have fought and how I have hurt her in lies and screaming fights. I grew up hunting, and upon reflection I draw connections to the sight of a white tail deer drawing its last breath as I do my mom's glassy eyed welled with tears. I think of the pain of survival, and the pain that comes in sustaining life. The pain of life is known no truer than to a mother.

In reflecting on nature and motherhood I am inspired by a creation story of the Hopi people who reside in what is now the American Southwest. The legend of the Spider Woman, also called Kokyangwuti and Grandmother Spider, recounts the creation of all things. In it, the Spider Woman's web connects all that she has created. She fashions animals and people from handfuls of mud and places them around the Earth, but she is not finished. She tasks her twin children to help her, saying:

> *"You are Pögánghoya. You are here to help keep this world in order*
> *when life is put upon it. Go now around all the world and put your*
> *hands upon the earth so that it will become solidified. This is your*
> *duty . . . You are Palöngawhoya. You are here to help keep this world*
> *in order when life is put upon it. This is your duty now: go about all*
> *the world and send out sound so that it may be heard throughout all*
> *of the land. When this is heard you will also be known as 'Echor for*
> *all sound echoes the Creator." (The Spider Woman and the Twins)*

Without the help of her children the ground is too unstable of her
creations to live and there are no "joyful sounds" in the air for them to
hear. Spider Woman has created the perfect world, but it is up to her
children to keep it that way.

From this I gather many things. It's a story about the interconnectivity
of all earthly fundamentals, of how the earth is divinely made up for
our dwelling and needs not the manipulation and maiming of colonial
thought form; but foremost, for me it is a story about two children
helping their mother. I am a twin myself, and in many ways, I see my
own mother in Spider Woman. My mother has created my world, but
it is up to me to steward it. The same can be said for our earth, who
provides for us all that we need, but it is up to us to understand the
fragile web of interconnectivity we balance on and reside in it accord-
ingly.

This theme of nature in correlation to motherhood is cemented in the
film *Land of Friends* in which a woman of Huila, Colombia describes the
sounds she heard when an energy company was drilling away rock to
erect dams, saying, "[m]other earth cries . . . I realized she is a woman
just like my mother and grandmother, as me and my daughter because
the way she moaned when they were chopping her to do the diverse
tunnels she roared in the same way one roars when giving birth" (Land
of Friends 2014). The idea that the earth is a mother is a common thread
amongst many ideologies of indigenous peoples; peoples who have
not forgotten the importance of respecting their environments because
these philosophies are intrinsic to their subsistence and longevity. The
Huila, for example, fight tooth and nail to protect their land because it

is not just land to them; the land is their mother. In connecting the land to the female body, their fight for land is to retain the very humanity which binds them to their motherland. Under this perspective, the fight is not about simply water, or crops, or fish but a fight for their very life and the prospective life to be sown on their ancestral soil.

In regards to the female body, artist Laura Aguilar reflects on the impact of her own body and nature. With many of her works being self-portraits with natural settings, she highlights the relationship between them. Not only does she draw parallels between her body and nature, but similarly the way the brown, female body and the earth are maimed and discarded by the "patriarchal, gendered, colonial paradigms in which we all live in" (Venegas 2018). In placing herself amongst a rough, rocky, and conventionally unsightly setting, she highlights her experience in a society in which her own form is regarded as unworthy and unattractive.

In providing this critique of white patriarchal ideals of body, nature, and beauty she also centers not just her experience but that of, "her half Irish, light-skinned mother Juanita, free-spirited grandmother Mary, great-grandmother Nasaria and great-great grandmother Antonia and back towards the ancient female lineage that goes before them" (Venegas 2018). Using images of her own body to tell her story, she tells the story of the women before her. Additionally, she tells the story of the greater mother, the earth, whose fate has been woven in a similar fashion to the female bodies of her ancestors. I see a resemblance in Aguilar's form laying across the earth akin the earth itself, who lays in solitude in the darkness of the cosmos. "As Aguilar bears witness to the untold stories and struggles of these women, unknown and invisible, as well as to her own story, they become us and we are all empowered in the process" (Venegas 2018).

Our earth, like a mother, serves as provider of anything one could ever need, but in an age of extraction this process is disrupted. What was once a delicate balance or interconnectivity, like a spider's web, is now fractured by borders, industry, resource extraction. I connect this to the Simon's Brick Company, which has supplemented this web for an artificial complex designed to suit all of its employees' needs. It includes housing, a school and a store, all necessities residents of the complex would typically have to leave for (Pérez 2022). Under the guise of convenience, Simon's Brick Company has created its own web architected in a fashion which urges employees to stay indentured to their work and to build up capital for an entity they will never see the fruit of. In disconnecting workers from place, they lose their ability to see value in moving elsewhere. Bound by the need to sustain their livelihood, residents are trapped within an artificial land which profits from their confinement. Denied access to natural spaces, Simon's Brick Company trapped employees in a new world, a moonscape of red earth, in efforts to separate them from the real thing.

So now, as I reflect on my own relationship with nature, I am brought back to the image of the Spider Woman. I imagine a web all around the earth, shrouding it like in Susan Boulet's painting *Spider Woman* (Figure 1). But unlike the painting, the web is no longer intact. It is tattered and overworked from decades of extraction and coloniality. Though designed perfectly, we have plucked bits of here and there and tried our best to make new worlds from the scraps, and now that our tactics prove faulty, what is there to do? I gather that we leave things as they are, use the web as intended instead of building false purposes and false worlds like we see in "Red Dust." I wonder, if we use what's around us as needed, and treat the rest as delicate as a spider's web will mother earth forgive us? Can she? This quandary is when I think of my own mother. In all the pain I have caused her, initially at my birth and the two decades that followed, I have always felt her embrace and undying devotion. I dream the same can be said for our world.

Spider Woman (Boulet)

Works Cited:

Boulet, Susan. *Spider Woman.*

Caycedo, Carolina. "Land of Friends, 2014. Descolonizando La Jagua." *Vimeo*, 2 Nov. 2022. https://vimeo.com/94685623.

Pérez, Nancy. "Red Dust: Migration and Labor as Seismic Fractures to the Anthropocene." *Resilience: A Journal of the Environmental Humanities*, 9.2, (2022): p. 14-29.

"The Spider Woman and the Twins." *Free Web Stats*, 2015, https://www.firstpeople.us/FP-Html-Legends/TheSpiderWomanandtheTwins-Hopi.html.

Venegas, Sybil. "Connected to the Land: The Work of Laura Aguilar." KCET, 11 April 2018.

Leslie & Poppy
Leslie Burkhart

Leslie Burkhart & California Poppy

Silencio
Noemi Gonzalez Maldonado

I am me, I am my mother, I am the countless other women who cannot or will not speak for themselves. In my weakness, solitude and confusion vivo por ella. La desterrada, la maldita, la cualquiera, ella que solo quiso salir adelante. Soy la hija maldita de mi madre, la que sin clase ni sangre pura puede desenmascarar al violador, al abusador, al pederasta que se topa solamente a la niña who does not know better, la niña who with her heart full of love, hope and dreams is an easy target for this pinche vida culera.

In many instances of my speech, the same questions in Español y English emerged. Why do you speak such harsh words? ¿No sabes tú que nuestro señor nos enseñó a perdonar y olvidar? It will only hurt you in the end, to hate and to rage so deeply, why can't you just seek love and peace?

Perhaps
Because as a person of color, I stopped fantasizing about a white knight in shining armor saving me and sweeping me off my feet. Perhaps because my daddy issues aren't the type to fantasize a man 20 years my senior but rather fantasize his power based on his skin tone.

Perhaps
Porque en la obra de mi poetisa favorita, *Para un Revolucionario,* la mujer es maldita y hechizada para siempre servir en la sombra de un hombre cuya pasión por la libertad no se extiende a "su casa" con la liberación de "su mujer."

Perhaps
I was meant to be my own rebelde not bajo las instrucciones del gran subcomandante insurgente Marcos.

Perhaps
Because I was full of rules instead of love. I knew a lady conocia her place, una señorita knew when to listen and when to callar; Note that una señorita was never allowed to speak out of turn, not that she ever had the mic.

Perhaps
I understood too well that little boys are taught by observation that a
woman is as disposable as their toys. Note: boys make war with their
toys.

Perhaps
It was the reason why I read poetry so much but I loved writing it
even more.

What does it mean to be me? Or you? To be?
Agotada, aferrada, trasnochada, adormecida y poderosa
To know family is the most important thing even if it's toxic. You
don't disrespect your father even if he has defiled and with his own
hands dishonored his own last name. I am a human descended from
gods and I am powerful. I am more than what my culture limits me,
more than what society restrains me, and so much more than I allow
myself to believe.

I'm Chicana, brown, and not at all the basic standard of beauty of
the states. I'm exotic, I'm a rarity and all who place their hands on
my hips think I would make a great bearer of children. My struggles
aren't my own, but rather that of countless other women that like me
stand in the shadows of men that cloud their thoughts. I understood
that my existence was resistance.

Resistance from the colonizer. Resistance to the pesticides force fed
to my mother while I was in her womb. Resistance from generational
trauma. I was a person, my own person. All flesh, blood, heart and
soul and no one could take that away from me. Resistance and yet
en mi comunidad de estudiante aunque yo sea "libre de crear mis
propios pensamientos" I am still indoctrinated, I am manipulated,
coerced, confused and drained of my finances. My heart beats agoniz-
ingly angry to be taught under a white institution en un mundo que
sirve al hombre blanco heterosexual, una mutación de genes incapaz
de sobrevivir la furia de Huitzilopochtli and the grand Olmec bird
monster ruler of the skies.

The need for lenguaje and words but the lack of iniciativa to speak
will leave my hermanas with a fist in their gargantas but I will not
be choked and perhaps un día soleado, quizás nublado, we can learn

about the way nuestras voces tiemblan y retumban. I will speak in my broken English, I will say *accept, tomorrow, community*, and *immigration* with my thick accent which passionately slips out reminding me who I am and where I come from. As if I am not already reminded that "it only comes out when you're angry" or "you cannot tell" that my first language is an inheritance of la conquista de Hernán Cortés.

I am passion, everything I do has a purpose.
I am loved.
I am loud, annoying, and unapologetic.
I am my mother's daughter.
La loca, la cínica, la descarada, la sinvergüenza.
La desvergonzada
La malcriada
La que nunca se calla
La que busca problemas
Perhaps
A boca cerrada no entran moscas
Pero… dios ayuda a la mujer que calla y obedece
Quizás
Yo no soy el titere to your puppeteer.
I am my mother's daughter yo digo lo que ella nunca dirá
I am the many things she refuses and denies.
Act II: Las apariencias engañan … y los sentimientos también.
Act I: was thinking saying nothing was better than speaking.
I am passion, reincarnation, love, rage, and indigenous, the last link to patriarchal servitude.

Take my house, Take my limbs, Take my womb, Take my land and my Tongue because with it I will build foundations of language and gouge out your eyes so within your hollow shell I can make a home for me, for my sisters, and my children. You can beat me, you can humiliate me, you can pluck out every last one of my hairs but you will never cut out my tongue with a dull blade forged with the hammer of injustice. I will keep Spitting, Spelling, Moving, and Making words and sentences for the Revival, Survival, Preservation and Growth of all my people. I am angry and you should be too.

Sueños / Dreams
Adrian Vielma Garcia

10 years have passed
since the last time
I've dreamed.
It is confusing
because
my parents have been dreaming
every day of their lives.
My parents thinking about what
their kid's future could be like
The American dream
was idealized for them,
but that was never
an option for me.

Una decisión,
costó mi sueño
de jugar deporte, mi carrera,
pero no me costó todo.
Disfrutar mi juventud
pensar que puedo hacerlo todo,
fue la única información que yo necesitaba
para tomar la decisión de salir sin permiso.
Ahora mi pie nunca volverá a ser el mismo
y mis sueños tampoco.

Racing down the hill
with my scooter,
feeling the wind hitting my face,
thinking I was invincible,
thinking I could do this every day,
until I hit a pothole.

Sentado en la banqueta
con sangre en mi pierna
Se me vino a mi mente,
todos los sueños que dejé en el suelo.

Lo bueno de todo esto
es que aún me quedan sueños,
aún puedo continuar
ayudando a las personas que lo necesitan.

El sueño en el suelo era de un niño
pero ahora ya es de un adulto.

Radical Futures
Isabela Escobedo

Over the course of the Radical Futures (CRGS 331) class, we have been exposed to numerous types of lifestyles, resistances, and artistic expressions that we would not normally have seen in generic education. This class enables us to learn about what various communities have in common and how they struggle in similar and different ways. This has helped to create a new perspective of connection within resistance and empowerment. The importance of and connection to land and water constantly comes into light, for it is what we all come from and something we all share.

Growing up in Seattle, Washington, water was always nearby. Driving 15 minutes East from my house was Lake Washington, where you could park your car one hundred feet away from the choppy water and watch boats go by. Then 15 minutes West from my parent's house is the Puget Sound, where the sunset behind the mountains makes the sky turn golden. I love that I grew up on the West Coast. I do not think I would want to live somewhere that does not have access to the ocean or some kind of body of water. The water in Seattle was always way too cold to actually go swimming in, but being on the beach with the sound of the waves is just as special. I did always love swimming in pools growing up. I still do, though I do not have the opportunity as often anymore. One of my all-time favorite things to do in the water was to let myself relax, float, and move *with* the water, and then watch the water catch light. A sense of calm but playful opportunity was just the right mix of rest and fun.

When I was in high school, I asked my Omi, my mom's mom, to write something for me to use in a school project. She wrote me a story about how she learned from her mom to swim in the Danube River. She has fond memories of her mother and sisters, "every bit like a mother duck, [we] would walk up the Danube, it seemed like miles, with [mother's] brood of five girls behind her, all of us in swimsuits, having left our towels and clothes and even shoes or sandals behind downstream..." (Hunt 2016). I have come to love this short and sweet story for many reasons, but one so especially because I have memories of swimming and water with her, similar to her with her own mother.

91

This semester at school, I participated in Danza Azteca. Among the many absolutely wonderful things about Danza Azteca, I think my top favorite part of the practice is that we usually dance with no shoes. The importance of all the elements in Danza Azteca creates a connection to the earth, and is an appreciation I hope to never lose. Danza helps me to feel connected, but I have not always felt so close to the earth around me, especially in my body. Photographer Suné Woods touches on nature and placement in relation to the natural body. Using her body and land together to disrupt dominant narratives of violence, Woods created the start of a much needed discussion for how space is seen. Kris Timken, author of "Suné Woods: Landscape and Memory," reminds us that belonging can come in any form we will it to. Much like Woods' counter narrative, photographer Laura Aguilar also utilizes the body and space in nature to disrupt internalized and embedded perceptions.

I was in awe when I first saw just a few of Aguilar's landscape photos. Specifically mentioned from the academic review by Sybil Venegas, titled "Take Me to the River," Laura Aguilar's work touches on land and belonging, as she places herself in scenes of nature with her body, mostly nude, as herself. She disrupts the dominant narratives that cloud the female, large, ethnic, and queer bodied individual. I have immense respect for women who choose to empower themselves by putting their bodies on platforms and into public media. I have had a long and not so healthy relationship with my body and everything it represents to me. I would say I am now at the healthiest I have been, and now within my own healing, but I hope one day I have healed enough to put my own body with nature as did Laura. Seeing Laura Aguilar's work helps me to heal further, for one, by being a representation I can connect to, and two, challenging me to continue my journey and respect my body and how I exist within it. My body is human and it is doing all it can for me to live my best life.

One component within healing that I find myself experiencing a lot is recognition, as part of healing is also acknowledging where you are now. I have done a lot of therapy in my life, and I could take up hours complaining about things I still struggle with or new issues that come along, but I have learned that it is also crucial to make time to stop and recognize (and maybe even celebrate) where you are in that moment. Even if I am not where I want to be, I am still in a different place than I was a year ago, in the same and different ways than 5 weeks ago, and even yesterday. Getting to learn about rocks in class, especially glacial erratics, has become a reminder of the importance of recognition, as every rock has a story, and none can lie about it.

Artist Beatriz Cortez and her work looks at human migration, and being in a place that is different from you. When I picture a glacial erratic I think about the surface of the rock, and the stories it tells of how it got there. The form of the glacial erratic, both naturally created and made by Cortez, show in texture their story of movement. Some parts of the surface may be smooth, but there are also bumps, cracks, broken bits, and even sometimes moss on an erratic glacier. Like laugh lines, tattoos, and scars, every body and vessel has a way of showing its physical journey through time.

Though glacial erratics are no longer migrating, they remind me of movement, rather than stagnance. They remind me that even though a process may be happening slowly, you are still moving, even if you can't really feel or see it happening. The earth is constantly spinning, and time is moving forwards, but it's happening so slowly and in such a way that we don't recognize it until after it has happened. Part of being a CRGS major includes considering and recognizing where I come from and how I got here. This has gotten me to think about the possibilities of location and how that plays a huge role for everyone. My mom's mother is from Germany, though my mom was born in Alaska. My dad was born in Coahuila, Mexico, but lived most of his school life in Texas, where he met my mom in college. They got married young and moved to Seattle, where I spent my whole life. Now, I have a Humboldt education that can help take me anywhere. In all the possible locations between countries, states, cities, and schools in my history and lineage, the universe aligned so that I would be here, now.

As a graduating senior, I have had to think a lot about my future, while simultaneously working at my present. When I think about where I want to be, I have no idea. When I think about where I am going, I think about Seattle, because that is my home, and where I will be living again. I love my home, but Seattle is not for me anymore. Seattle is big, busy, and future-oriented. I like to have slow mornings, quiet walks, and be present-minded. Even though Seattle is where I was born, I have never felt a huge connection to the physical land. Being a CRGS major makes me have more consideration for where I am, and has also given me better resources to understand the history of where I live.

When I took a geology class in high school, my teacher did a small unit on glacial erratics. I do not remember a lot, but I do recall the opportunity to get extra credit to go take a selfie with the local glacial erratic rock, located right in the middle of a Seattle neighborhood. That rock is a landmark for people in the local area. I remember growing up and kids would spend time climbing and playing on it. I believe I was twelve when I first climbed the erratic. Having that memory, combined with what I have been learning about and discussing recently, connects several years in my life, from 2016 to now. I recall having printed out the picture of my selfie with the erratic, and my teacher promptly stuck it on the whiteboard for all the class to see. I am unable to find that image again, but maybe I will take the opportunity to remake it.

In Seattle, I will be in Duwamish region and in a county originally named for a slave-owning white man. Though now it is widely advertised that King County realigned its brand under the namesake of Martin Luther King Jr., these histories are not yet talked about enough, if even at all in Seattle, and that does make me a little nervous. But, like an erratic glacial rock, I will be in a place a bit different from what I have been used to, but my presence is the first of many steps to have CRGS celebrated and respected the way we do erratic glaciers. Who knows? My future is as radical as I make it.

Works Cited:

Anonymous. "Background about the Logo- King County." *Background about the Logo- King County*, Dec. 2016.

LaCava, Stephanie, et al. "Beatriz Cortez: 'Drawing Lines in the Air with Metal'." *Frieze*, 24 Sept. 2020,

Hunt, I. "Learning to Swim, Dangerously." 2016, Ft. Collins, Colorado.

Timken, Kris. "Suné Woods: Landscape and Memory." *The New Explorers*, Sept. 2015.

Venegas, Sybil. "Take Me to the River: The Photography of Laura Aguilar" in Epstein, Rebecca (ed.), *Laura Aguilar: Show and Tell* (2017). UCLA Chicano Studies Research Center Press.

Venegas, Sybil. "Connected to the Land: The Work of Laura Aguilar." KCET, 11 April 2018.

Xelfi
Namixtu'lú' Esteva

Understanding My New Normal
Brianna Juarez

I am a Chicana in higher education.

I am in some ways privileged and some ways not.

There are many intersections of myself that scream oppression, that exude trauma, that are fueled in fear, but this wasn't existent in my paradigm in what I previously thought of to be my *formative years*.

I am a queer, first-generation, Mexican American woman living in Northern California. I am not from here, I am from Southern California; a place where having all these identities never made me feel othered. Growing up in SoCal meant a lot of things, such as actually seeing the sun every day, looking to my left or right, and seeing people who looked like me. People who spoke in my mother's native tongue that I grasped tiny portions of, people who I felt safe with even if I didn't know them. I always lived in the hood, sometimes my hood was "nicer" than other hoods but still the hood nonetheless. The ghetto bird flew above my home countless nights, and yet I still felt safe.

I didn't start to feel unsafe in my own home until I moved to Northern California. I could no longer look to my left or to my right and see those who looked like me, or looked like other BIPOC. I had to search in a sea of whiteness that felt endless. I began to lose myself in this whiteness. I began to feel the oppression and trauma that was there all along besides me but wasn't prevalent because I had been privileged, shielded, and fooled that it had skipped me.

Silly me.

I am a Chicana in higher education in a predominantly white area that I do *not* feel safe in. I am a Chicana residing in an area that had Trump parades on Sunday afternoons. That was normal, but it was not **my** normal, or was it? What is my new normal?

My normal used to be living in a home filled with my mother's love and my father's pride. Now my normal is living in a home with my partner's love, pride, and my kitties' silly selves. My normal used to be waking up to a home cooked meal that my mother would sometimes resentfully make but I didn't taste the resentment, mostly because it was not meant for me, I just tasted the love. Now my normal is cooking my own food and trying my best to fill it with love and not the stress, pain or trauma that I sometimes think is oozing out of me. My normal used to be hanging out with my cousin and friends every weekend, doing nothing and everything, but having the time of my life. Now my normal is working, studying, living, spending time with my partner when it fits into our schedules, and mostly feeling alone. You see, I don't have many friends in Humboldt, maybe that's because of lack of effort on my end but for the most part I would say it's because I never felt like I belonged. Community was never something I had to search or yearn for. Previous to living in NorCal, I was a part of my community, there was no searching for it, there was no wondering if I fit in, I just felt **in.** But now, where do I fit in?

I am a Chicana in higher education living in Northern California.

Up until my senior year working on my Bachelor's degree, I never felt like my institution loved me as much as I loved it - an unrequited love, a toxic love. A love that was so consuming, at times I thought it was destroying me.

I am a Chicana in higher education who is wrapping up my B.A. in Philosophy. This subject never felt like I belonged in it, I knew this, I knew that it was not a field meant for women *especially **not** women of color.* I knew this, and being who I am, and who I was raised to be, I did not care and pursued the degree. What I didn't know was that it was going to break who I was.

Countless courses and countless lessons excluded my existence and when it accounted for it, it was romanticized or demonized which forced me to feel on the outskirts of the information. How can I truly study and be connected with the information? I felt ostracized and honestly, really sad because of this. I could no longer hide under my shielded existence; I felt an uprise within myself. I told myself I was working on my degree in philosophy so I could become a professor and be the representation I never had. But that never felt easy or natural, it felt like I would be living in a cycle of repeated trauma. It was because of this that I became cynical.

Kathy Pero Like Katí
Kathy Zamora

Es mi último semestre en Cal Poly Humboldt. Tengo muchas emociones con la idea de graduarme. Decidí a tomar una clase de español porque me imagino usando mis skills, mis habilidades como social worker o educator, con mi gente, hispanohablantes. Desde niña, mi relación con la lengua español ha cambiado. En mi vida, hablo Spanglish, mainly English, y con mi abuelita solamente español. Aunque el autor, Richard Rodriguez, como segunda generación nos recuerda que tenemos "el derecho y la obligación de hablar el lenguaje público de los gringos," ser bilingüe nace nuestra identidad bicultural. Ahora estoy reclamando mi lengua, yo soy bilingüe, bicultural, Chicana, and I love it.

El español fue mi primer lenguaje, y es la lengua que escucho cuando estoy en casa o en la casa de mis tíos. Crecí con primxs y nos platicamos en Spanglish. Como hija que también es first-gen student, tengo una perspectiva de la cultura Mexicana y de Estados Unidos. Mis padres son de un pueblito, Santa Monica, Puebla México, y yo y mis hermanos nacimos aquí. Crecí escuchando a mis padres decirme: "Este es tu país" o "Cuando comemos en la mesa, se habla español." Mi mamá exigía que hablemos español, para que no se pierda la lengua de mi familia. Sin embargo, Richard Rodriguez, notó que estar en el espacio público se refiere a hablar la lengua de más prestigio. Estoy de acuerdo con esto porque mis abuelos hablaban Náhuatl, pero en la escuela no era la 'lengua de más prestigio,' forzando monocultura del español en Puebla. Los maestros pegaron a mis padres para que solamente hablaran español basada en el racismo anti-indigena en México. Igualmente aquí, en Estados Unidos la asimilación a una lengua, especialmente el inglés, perpetúa una cultura en los Estados Unidos de monocultura, tratando de eliminar la diversidad de lenguajes indígenas. Aunque tristemente, ser bicultural en una escuela de ingles alteró mi relación con mi lengua, encontré mi comunidad, con los que se identifican como Chicanos, first-generation students, or other personas de color.

Como hija menor, yo tuve la oportunidad de hablar el inglés con mis hermanitos. Mi lengua cambio and I mainly spoke English. El español fue muy difícil para mí until I enrolled into Spanish classes in high school. Me gustaría decir que mi español ha mejorado y estoy muy orgullosa. Aunque, yo y mis hermanos hablamos más en inglés. Como Richard Rodriguez menciona, el español se habla en la casa. It wasn't until classes de CRGS (Critical Race, Gender, and Sexuality Studies), Ethnic Studies, Native American Studies, me dieron las herramientas y perspectiva para entender mi identidad, y mi relación con el español, ser Chicana y bicultural. Afortunadamente, mi educación me dio la historia de mi gente, y la energía de reclamar mi valor, mi cultura, y mi lengua.

De 21 años reflejó la experiencia de mi niñez comparada con la de mis padres. Miro todos los sacrificios que ellos tenían que hacer para que yo pudiera obtener higher educación. Esto es lo que ellos imaginaron por mí. Desde cuándo, mi mamá exigía que hablara español. Ella entendía que ser bilingüe es poderoso: ofrece más oportunidades de trabajo o carreras. Estoy reclamando la lengua de mis padres, mis familiares, aunque no hablamos Náhuatl, la lengua de mis abuelos. Me río del irony de que cuando era niña de ocho años me dio pena hablar el español afuera de la casa. Ahora en mi último año de la universidad estoy trabajando en una escuela que practica inmersión de español, y me aseguré estar en una clase de español. Dicho esto, me recuerdo de mi mamá. Como ella dice, "La vida va en rondas." Yo trabajo en el Children 's Center, cuidando bebes, y por mucho tiempo ese fue el trabajo de mi mamá. Cuidaba a babies, niños de elementary o mis primos. Y ahora yo estoy trabajando con niños de 3 meses hasta 10 años, practicando mi español meanwhile fortaleciendo mi cultura.

En fin, estoy agradecida de que mi mamá llamó la atención por ser bilingüe. Le doy gracias por sus sacrificios, y su cariño porque ella me ha apoyado en mis estudios y mi identidad de ser Chicana. Más que nada, extraño la voz de mi mamá. Extraño como dice mi nombre, "Katí." Extraño escuchar el español de mi mamá, es más que una lengua que tiene un "estándar." Al contrario, la lengua es una gran parte de nuestra identidad, no es algo que se puede criticar como incorrecto. Ser bilingüe y tener la magia de poder hacer code switching, es ser bicultural.

Rooted Home
Olie M. Espinoza

Para Mi Papa, Que Sigue Viviendo En El Mar
Melissa Torres Escalante

I suffer from something called aphantasia, the inability to see/picture/ imagine things in my mind. This doesn't stop me from knowing what things look like, I can describe fruits, people, and things well. When you close your eyes and imagine a red star, what do you see? Can you see the shape of a star? The color? Or do you only see an outline? When I try to do this task, I see nothing. It's just black with a gray static overlay, like a 90s tv that has just been turned off. The lack of ability to see things in my head has never bothered me before, the fact that when I close my eyes all I see is blackness and static. But now I live my days feeling as if I am meant to suffer. Now, when I close my eyes, no matter how hard I plead with a god that never listens, I can't see my dad. No matter how many details I know, no matter if I repeat his features like I'm praying the rosario, I can only see him in pictures.

Even now as I write this, I recall everything I can. His curly hair that refused to fall from his head even in his 70s, the black that faded to gray and white, the serious and impossible to read facial expression, his nose and how it looks so much like my own, his eyes that could never decide between hazel and green. And as much as I try to remember him alive, the details of his death bed creep forward the most. I can't remember my dad alive without remembering him dead.

My dad loved to fish, that's how he survived going hungry in El Salvador after being orphaned as a child during the 60s. But when he came here to the States, fishing was no longer a survival tactic. It was a way for him to remember his home, to remember his family and friends that he could no longer speak to, to relax and let go. He loved the ocean even more. As he got older and slowed down more than he would like to admit, he would say "preocupanse cuando ya no quiero ir al mar, cuando no quiero pescar."

Out of my siblings, there's 3 of us with me included, I am the one who picked fishing up with the same passion. My brother was born 14 years before me and raised in El Salvador by my grandmother; he never got the chance to experience having parents because they were in a completely different country sending money back. My little sister, 3 years younger than me, just didn't like it. The beach was too cold, too windy, she wanted to go home and sleep. Then there was me, the child who ran to the sea as if it was my long-lost family. My parents first took me to the beach to fish when I was only a couple of months old and since then they have taken me. I remember being small, I couldn't look over the wooden railings of the pier and watching my dad with wide eyes as he got his fishing rods ready. From setting up the hooks, putting on the weights, and lastly hooking the pieces of bait. Finally, there was the way he cast the rod, the fishing line flying through the air with such a force and speed that I was sure it would snap and get lost in the waters below. But it never did, not when he had to reset his bait, not when he began to catch fish. I remember in those moments wanting to grow and be as tall as him, just so that I could finally fish by his side.

It took several years but I had to have been around 9 when my dad began to teach me, first by explaining everything that he was doing. Then by letting me reel in the rods whenever there was a bite, or it was time to check the bait. After several months, it was time for me to cast my first fishing rod. It went terrible. Being inexperienced, I wasn't confident to send it flying the way he did from the pier. But slowly, I began to gain that confidence. In the beginning, I tried to will the fish to take my bait, to get stuck onto my hook so that I could show my dad that I did it. My impatience made me fidgety, had me checking every few minutes. "Con paciencia se hace todo," was what he would tell me. I think it took me around a year to finally settle down. And during this time, especially during the summer months, my dad and I would spend every single Friday there at Newport Beach pier, fishing and not saying a word. There was a language that we developed together, one that didn't involve speaking to be understood. He taught me how to read the tides, how certain fish come out during the day, how to catch sand crabs so we could have live bait.

My father was a quiet man, steady like the earth. As a child, he lost so much and from a young age he was never allowed to enjoy the comforts of being a kid. I recognize that due to his life experiences, he was never a man of words, rather expressing what he felt through actions. A typical Latino dad, I mentioned once that I loved Sabritones and for weeks afterwards he would buy me a bag every time he went to Northgate. His actions were plenty, although there were moments in the silence that we shared that I craved to hear words. What did he think about? What were his dreams when he was a boy? What was it that made him decide to come to this country? There were so many questions that whirlpooled in me and yet there was nothing that he wanted to share, always keeping his emotions and thoughts close. In that aspect, he was like the ocean, profound and full of the unknown.

I am a fisherman's daughter. There were times that I even began to catch more than he did, when I could tell where the fish were and aim well. There is a unique culture around pier fishing, especially when it's the same group of people seeing you every week. There was a time when one of my dad's fishing friends came over after I caught several fish and asked my dad about me fishing. All I heard my dad say was "La estudiante ya pasó a su maestro." My chest filled with pride, carried forth by happiness like swell waves.

At times, I miss the sea, the ocean and its secrets. We stopped going the moment the pandemic had us in lock down. Yet, there was mi viejo, watching YouTube videos about fishing and constantly setting up his equipment. "Cuando ya podemos, vamos ir a pescar." He would tell me. Enthusiastically, I would nod my head, looking forward to being able to fish the way we used to. In the end, that day never came. I can still feel the screams in my chest building up, like a tsunami about to reach the shore. The day that my dad passed was the day I knew I would never find another person to fish with again. I still don't have the heart to, can't find the will to go by myself. Perhaps I will someday, when the pain and the grief doesn't feel like a current that wants to take me under and drown.

Chapter 4
Verano : Summer

Up River Coyote
Emmanuel Pihneefich Cyr

Humboldt County is also home several Native American tribes; The Karuk Tribe, Hupa Tribe, Yurok Tribe, and the Wiyot Tribe. I grew up in a town named Willow Creek, found in North Eastern Humboldt County. Willow Creek is considered aboriginal territory for the Hupa Tribe. Willow Creek's rich history was developed during the gold rush. Historically, during the gold rush era, Willow Creek was formerly known as "China Flat" because it was conceived as a huge concentration camp of Chinese people who as slaves were forced to work mining claims and build roads. Tourists today come to the area to look for the legend of Bigfoot; the famous bigfoot sighting known as the Patterson Film was taken only 40 miles away from Willow Creek. When I was a kid, I always remember going to the famous Bigfoot parade, as a tradition every summer, with my family to celebrate Bigfoot's presence as a community. Humboldt County as you all may know is also known for being home to the marijuana industry, and during the fall you can see many "trimmigrants" arrive in my community.

Growing up, I would experience several instances that provided me a sense of belonging. The most memorable ones would be my daily commute from my home to my school or families houses on the Hoopa Valley Reservation, where my mom, a Karuk tribal member, has taught at the elementary school for 20+ years. My commute consisted of a 15-mile drive through the bluffs of the Six Rivers National Forest following the Trinity River. I would always stare out the window watching the river contact the rocks and would use the river as a way to tell what time of the year it was based on the flows. I would go onto the reservation to see my grandma and my brothers' families and hang out with my peers, cousins, aunties, uncles, and grandparents. The river was like the highway for my community, and during summers we would follow the river upstream and downstream to participate in our cultural ceremonies including the brush dances and flower dances. My sister's flower dance was very memorable for my family, where my whole community came together for her and womanhood, and the legacy that she now carries as a Karuk woman.

Being present in my culture, it was important to me to have access to fishing and hunting to provide for my family but also to engage in activities that became a part of my identity today. I think of the river and the mountains when I think of home. Driving around with my dad in his pickup, early morning deer hunting, watching the world around me go from dark to light and feeling anticipation was one of my favorite places of belonging. Native/cultural foods have always been a way I have been able to connect with my community as well. My mother would cook salmon for dinner at least 2 times a week; everyone I knew in my close community could relate! Salmon, huckleberries, my grandmas' homemade biscuits and a big pot of beans and canned deer meat are food items that make me feel a sense of home.

My native community has faced many challenges throughout colonization. Genocide, boarding school, cultural assimilation, ecological destruction is to name a few. We've had people try to take so much from us, everything, from our lives to our identity and the things that are most important to our culture. My tribe, the Karuk Tribe, is centered in the Mid-Klamath Watershed. Our people have experienced, many forms of genocide throughout colonialization and during the goldrush. My mother, grandmother, and great grandmother all attended boarding school as children. My people today are federally recognized yet we have very little rights to the land we have occupied for centuries. The hardships my people and other local tribes have gone through are reflected throughout my community. I see it when I think of the prominent alcohol, and drug abuse, and by witnessing local people stuck on the reservation dependent on welfare, and commodities is a direct representation of genocide that have created an endless cycle for many people in my community. However, although we find struggles, I also see people from my community coming together to find strength from all these challenges and bring healing even though the worst of times have taken place. To me, I felt the photo essay," "The River Remembers" by Laura Aguilar showed some relevant themes of decolonization throughout her work. A quote that I thought stood out states," Aguilar's nude self-portraits demonstrate that colonized bodies of color, like the land, can be sites of healing as well as sites of artistic regeneration." By her showing this kind of work it reflected to me the uncomfortable feeling that takes place when recognizing decolonization to the human body and the surrounding land.

To me and my community, our natural resources and local traditions are what are most important to us. The salmon that run up the streams are the most important source of food that my communities have always depended upon. The resources and local wisdom is the prominent reason native American people are so resilient. Everything is connected, from the grasses and trees, to the animals and fish, and the fire and snow on the landscape. It is important for me to make this connection because as a community we all share this same mindset. A quote from the article titled, "Ecocide is Genocide" by Lauren Eichler states a perfect representation of the importance resources are to Native people, "during the 2016-17 Standing Rock movement against the Dakota Access Pipeline, Native American protestors held signs that stated, "Water is sacred" and "Water is life." These posters did more than signify the fear that a resource would be affected. These words signified a concern about the wellbeing, health, and livelihood of the water and land for its own sake as an integral member of the community."

The way that me and my community pass down knowledge and histories is from storytelling. One of my favorite things to do is to sit by the fire with an elder in my community and to listen to what they say, through their local wisdom and knowledge you can come to learn a lot. My community uses stories to understand creation, landmarks, feelings of love and anger, lessons, etc. Everything is in the surrounding environment has a story of why it is the way it is and its connection to places/beings. My favorite character in many of my local stories is the coyote, in most stories he's the trickster, always getting himself into trouble learning most lessons the hard way. Most people in my community question my parents' decision to name me after him. My middle name is, "Pihneefich" which means coyote in Karuk. Although I can understand how ironic it can be. I have grown to accept the coyote's persona and take it with me when going about in this big world from lesson to lesson.

Works Cited:

Eichler, Lauren J. "Ecocide Is Genocide: Decolonizing the Definition of Genocide." *Genocide Studies and Prevention*, vol. 14, no. 2, 2020, pp. 104–121., https://doi.org/10.5038/1911-9933.14.2.1720.

Fragoza, Carribean. "The River Remembers Laura Aguilar." *Aperture*, Special Edition: Latinx, Issue 245, Winter 2021.

agua bendita
Jessica Aguirre

You have to harbor a good amount of trust within you to let yourself float on a flowing river. It took me years to build that confidence. This thought crossed me as I lay afloat the Mad River. I looked over at my coworker that I invited to spend a river day with me, and wondered at what age did she learn how to swim? I'm brought to my senses when she splashes me and challenges me to competition. She beats me across the river, and as she pulls herself out of the water in a celebratory chant, I plunge underneath the water in joy because that was the first time I gracefully swam without any fear or anxiety. I've signed up for swimming classes that I never showed up to, I've had every excuse in the book written out in a doctor's note for P.E. classes, I've skipped out on many river days to avoid being swept away by a current. I refused to voluntarily enter any body of water until I was 21 years old.

I like to blame my lack of water placements in my birth chart for an explanation to my fear of water. In reality, there may be two reasonable answers to the apprehensiveness I swim through–generational trauma and climate change. I was born in Ogden, Utah. It's this little ghost town that I existed in for two years. We then moved 12 hours away to the hot Central Valley of California. My father wanted to be closer to his mother, my grandmother, who may rest in peace. Without any context, I grew up an only child even though I had four older siblings–until I was 7. My parents both came from broken marriages when they decided to elope and escape from their lives in Utah. This resulted in a strained relationship with my older sisters from my dad's side and a distant connection with my brother from my mom's. The only sibling living with my parents and I was my sister, Beatriz. We're ten years apart, so we were never close growing up. Our first years in California are a blur to me; my three core memories consist of my 5th RBD birthday party, my sister moving out at 16, and the small kiddie pool my mom bought at the local Foods CO.

Living in Tulare, California is not a thrill for all. Like any 17-year-old moving away from their hometown I vowed to never return. There was nothing that can bring me back, especially after experiencing more welcoming communities. This was my mentality leaving. My thoughts have definitely matured after reflecting on my relationship with my mother and father. My reluctance in returning back home boils down to my stolen childhood. When my sister moved, my mom and her both ended up pregnant around the same time. I was getting ready for school one winter morning. December mornings in Tulare are foggy and dense, you can barely see past six feet. I was running to our living room to check the PBS channel just in case my school bus route was canceled. Before I was able to turn the TV on I heard a loud yell coming from the kitchen. Concerned, I slowly walked into the room thinking someone was robbing us again but all I saw was my mom bent over the sink, clutching her stomach. There is this clear liquid running down her legs. She's yelling at me to call my sister so she can take her to the hospital because her 'water broke'. What water? I thought she was carrying my baby brother in her stomach? I was so confused but my mind went into autopilot and the rest was a blur. Within the next hour I was in my classroom taking my spelling test and all I could write was water. I was scared and upset; I didn't see my family for a week. I was being taken care of by my mom's coworker Rosa. The week spent with Rosa I learned so much about babies. She taught me how to change a diaper using my stuffed teddy bear and I was able to properly make a baby bottle. Rather than learning how to swim or ride a bike I was preparing to take on responsibilities meant for adults. I didn't realize all of this preparation was going to dictate the rest of my childhood.

Upon this specific reflection I can no longer sit here and hold resentment towards my parents. It wasn't their fault that they had to work long hours and had no one to look after their new born. My mom had to return to work after two weeks. Which is insane to me! Her poor body, she JUST gave birth. I respect the solitude she chose when she would get home. I respect the long hour baths after work. Suné Woods' "Landscape and Memory" photo collection reminds me of my mother. My mother deserves to properly heal her body after giving life. Denying brown and black bodies a way of living that is fulfilling is damaging in so many aspects. We deserve to feel whole with ourselves and nature. Reimagining my mother in a space where she can be playful and a place where she can rest and heal is a sequence, I wish she could fully envelope herself. It's something I'm working to give to her, and I can only do that by returning home.

I spent half of my summers with my cousins in Utah; it was a good break from the scorching heat of Tulare. My brother would take us hiking to beautiful waterfalls and spring waters. Thankfully the ponds in these areas were shallow and the deeper ends were kind of a struggle to get to. Regardless, my brother always insisted on taking a dip in the waters and I always fought with him because I did not want to get in. Everyone, including the adults, would gang up on me and shame me. *You don't know how to swim? Don't you live in California? Aren't there beaches where you live? You're not a real Californian...* I wasn't having fun. I turn to my sister-in-law and see her rocking my niece side to side. I walk over to them and ask to hold her so my sister-in-law can join everyone in the water. I play with my niece and protect her from the water. A role that will remain with me every time we go to the rivers (Fig.1).

Although my hatred of water was well understood among my family members, they would still invite me to river days. Majority of the drive to the river included threats of being thrown into the water because everyone in my family 'learned' how to swim by being chucked into the water and choosing to swim instead of drowning. Which seemed so illogical to me because how will I *know*, how will I *choose* to swim back up? How can I trust my family members to save me if I do start drowning? What if we both start drowning and it's all because of me? The pressure was too much. I rather choose to sit back with my mother who told me the horrors of water currents. As she tells me about her experiences of drowning–very morbid, I know– I admire how silly her descriptions can be. But I just laugh and promise her I won't go in without a life vest.

I kept the promise I made to her. No matter how ridiculous I looked with floaties. The rare times I did join my friends to the river I didn't feel ashamed knowing that I couldn't swim. They made me feel comfortable and even promised me swimming lessons. Yet I was unable to shake my mom's promise even when I was missing out on all of the fun. That all changed when I suffered from a traumatic pelvic injury that strained my lower back. My physical therapist recommended I swim at least twice a week to alleviate back pain. I refused for two years. I'm still in disbelief that I chose agonizing pain over a swimming lesson. My friends watched as I struggled with an exaggerated bent back and decided to confront me and my fear of water. With their help I learned how to comfortably hold my breath underwater, without obstructing the airflow in my nostrils, which caused me to swallow all of the water. I thank them every day for their patience and kindness.

*A trip to the Wild Waters waterpark. I watch over my
nieces and nephews as they eat fruits and snacks.*

Central Valley heat is no joke. The valley has been suffering from historic drought for decades. Tulare was once the largest freshwater lake in the west, but due to greedy irrigation and climate change the area has been left empty and open for farming made possible through the groundwater still available. This water crisis affected our day to day lives. Like many other areas of California, Tulare had strict water usage laws to preserve water. Communities were allowed water usage on certain days based on the last number of your street address. My address ends with an odd number so we were assigned Tuesday and Thursday to use our water. Although every house in the neighborhood I lived in was granted specific watering days, my father took notice of certain privileges our counter-white neighbors held when he was cited for a leaking hose and the vecina next door was watering during the weekends. My father understood, not in these specific terms, that moving his family to this suburban adjacent community was not got to be his American dream but instead how Jose Esteban Muñoz describes the way our "brownness can be known by tracking the ways through which global and local forces constantly attempt to devalue and diminish their verve" (Muñoz, 1). Either way, his flores were going to be the brightest on the block.

As I see things, our relationship with waterways, land, and other forms of nature can be spiritually and physically healing. Putting in work to understand yourself and the world surrounding you can bring much harmony and a sense of peace we seem to be missing today. Our own fears and anxieties can limit beautiful connections that may bring forth a fulfilling life.

Works Cited:

Aguirre, Jessica. Figure 1: Photograph of Jessica and three nephews and niece at the waterpark. 15, June, 2013.

Muñoz, José Esteban. "Brown Commons" in Chambers-Letson and Nyong'o (eds.), *The Sense of Brown* (2020). Duke University Press. pp.1-7.

Timken, Kris. "Suné Woods: Landscape and Memory." *The New Explorers*, 22 Sept. 2015. http://thenewexplorers.com/land-scape-and-memory/ Accessed 15 Dec. 2022.

Our Connection
By Maria Citlalli Rodriguez

When I was a child, my parents would regularly take me to Jalisco, Mexico where we would indulge in the culture and the beautiful connections with our friends and family. I attain memories of myself being taken to the local community binario, feeling full of love as I slip down the little water slides into the arms of my father. Being there with all my aunts, uncles and cousins, it's wonderful to be in that space surrounded by family as the sweet sensation of the water presses on me while the sun acts as mediator. This is what I knew to be true about my community, that it is everything to us and when I am in the comfort of my hometown, it is almost like I never left, like my family never had to migrate. I see in my great aunts and my estranged cousins how they really connect to me and I connect to them and the world around beneath us. I know that as a child, I was safe to fling myself down a water slide and know that my father was at the bottom ready to catch me from the water and save me.

I learned about the various ways that communities connect to each other as well as their environments. Representation very much matters when we live in a patriarchal capitalist society and it's so imperative that we can connect to each other in meaningful ways that disrupt everything we are "supposed" to act or be like. It was great to learn about the *Secret Gardens* and the history that comes with that. Rachel Aima does a deep dive on the *Seeds of Change* installments that Maria Thereza Alves put together of different indigenous plants found all over the cities, stranded by a New York shipping past that isn't one we can forget. "Like people, seeds can unexpectedly find themselves far from their homelands", which is what happened to the people forced to come into this so-called free country (Aima, 99). These seeds that laid dormant for many years started springing up and to me, this symbolized colonized populations and how they too, had to withstand and endure oppressive forces. The plants flourish like how people do and the ballast flora serves as a reminder towards the unjust and violent history that comes from the "pre-colonial period that shipping and transport infrastructure effaced"(Aima, 100). The point is that the seeds remember, they know that the land was stolen from the Lenape peoples and they know that Wall Street is built on a historical African burial ground. The seeds remember.

Exploring the idea of having a space where Brown people are valued and listened to is very important, there are many ways that communities tend to come together. Laura Aguilar is exceptional and revolutionary because she allowed me to place myself in an unapologetic lens living as a Latina who has internalized a sense of shame for being plus-sized. I know in my heart that this shame stems from years and years of western beauty practice being shoved down my throat. It's refreshing to see Aguilar in her element as someone who can represent me and others who feel like me. She had difficulty expressing herself verbally because of auditory dyslexia but was able to take comfort in photography. She is known for using herself as a subject to confront and rebel against the subjected Mexican American female identity. Her nude self-portraits are re-imaginative of photography because she is able to place herself in a landscape and feel free from the bonds of a disempowered large brown female body while embracing the ruggedness that nature has to offer, allowing herself to surrender.

Raquel Gutierrez highlighted the importance of Rafa Esparza's art which broke through the bounds of what revolutionary artists can do. One of his projects *Bust, a Meditation on Freedom* was achieved by using a single sledge hammer and a small chisel to "bust" himself out of a concrete wall to further convey the marginalization and assimilation that communities are forced to go through. Each hammer bang "became an ancestral homing device aimed at the masculine utterance of self, starved for airspace inside the state's impervious walls" (Gutierrez, 1). The exhibitions and performances by this man were used as an instrument to carve out space that wasn't there for people of color in the first place. The use of gender in his work challenged the social constructions of Mexican masculinity while also adhering to the oppression he feels in the States as a Hispanic person. With this type of spatial art for Brown people, there's this concept of subverting power and therefore allowing us to envision a future where we all can coexist or at least thrive under the pressures of hetero-patriarchal dominance. As Gutierrez states, "Power- like energy, either static or kinetic-always assumes different positions" (2016, 2). I can rationalize a future where there is space carved out for Brown and Black people, despite all that this country has done for their marginalized communities.

For too long, I learn about the hardships that my friends and family have had to endure as Brown people and all the nastiness that comes with the imperialism of the world. It was my first year in Humboldt and I experienced what is known as "culture shock" by the amount of White individuals around me. More so seeing how some people acted when coming from a place of privilege and shelter. As a Brown person myself, I found comfort in being able to surround myself with people who are more like me, a place where I can feel safe and seen. That feeling came from being able to use some of the few resources like the Educational Opportunities Program (EOP) and from the Critical Race, Gender and Sexualities Department. The community that came from these resources made me feel like I belonged there and I deserved to be here. Jose Esteban Muñoz was able to channel this idea of carving out space for Brown folk in *The Sense of Brown* when explaining the topic of *The Brown Commons*. We all have environments from which we thrive better and Munoz understands that, given the violent history of the United States towards Brown people. A space for people of color is a great deal as it allows the community of otherwise devalued people to find themselves in something greater than themselves. The Brown Commons is significant because it was born out of the radicality of Black power and student movements who collectively refuse to be subjected to "dominant logics and systems of thought" and move towards understanding that we all have more in common than we think (Muñoz, 3). Knowledge production in areas like Ethnic studies is nothing to take lightly because many people are finally starting to see themselves in history and therefore uncovering this manifest destiny for what it truly is, which is a system meant to favor those in power. There is an urgency in the air to dismantle a system that has done nothing but cause harm to the planet and its inhabitants. Muñoz argues, "that the world is and has always been Brown and has been so despite the various blockages that keep us from knowing or being attuned to brownness" (2020, 3), revitalizing that the Brown commons is an attempt to bring people together to find a commonality in our struggles of having to withstand various oppressive factors in their environments. In a sense, showing Brown people that they are not alone and they never will be.

Connections to the land and to yourself are essential to the diaspora of having to assimilate. A commonality that comes from these attempts of reconnecting to the land is the creative emotionality that comes with wanting to be free. Activists are artists in their own right. A few years back, I traveled back to that little town in Jalisco where my dad grew up and visited the binario, which was that waterpark that I loved so much as a young girl. I went with my cousins and some aunties on a summer day where there was probably just one more family out enjoying themselves. My senses were all warm since I was in a familiar place and I felt safe. I can relate this to being in a Brown commons as we found each other as a community in this location that held many years of fond memories. Looking back, I can see it was because I *was* in a familiar place, a place where I had been many times before, only I hadn't recognized it. The feeling however, was refreshing as I was able to feel like I was a kid again, somewhere where I used to play. It's in these spaces filled with ancestral love that I feel the most connected to myself and to the earth that I walk on every day.

Works Cited:

Aima, Rahel. "Secret Gardens: Rahel Aima on Maria Thereza Alves Seeds of Change." (2018). Artforum International.

Gutiérrez, Raquel. "Rafa Esparza: How Brown Matters in the Multiplicity of Presence" in Moshayedi A, Walker H (eds.) *Made in LA: a, the, though, only.* (2016). Munich, London, New York: DelMonico Books.

Muñoz, José Esteban. "Brown Commons" in Chambers-Letson and Nyong'o (eds.), *The Sense of Brown* (2020). Duke University Press. pp.1-7.

Venegas, Sybil. "Take Me to the River: The Photography of Laura Aguilar" in Epstein, Rebecca (ed.), *Laura Aguilar: Show and Tell* (2017). UCLA Chicano Studies Research Center Press.

The Puzzle of Me
Matt Aung

My blood runs through borders
Eclectic in my DNA, I represent a lineage
of cultures, vast and diverse
My face is that of generations
past, present, future.

Yet the blood that makes me
is muddled in mystery and confusion
Disconnected from my tribe,
navigating foreign lands searching for
a piece of me lost to
time, fate, destiny.

I am from the land anew, the world of old,
and eastern temples
Out west, I'm bounded skywards
Breaking through the Earth, I return
to the land I come from…

Fruit Salad
Nayali Abarca

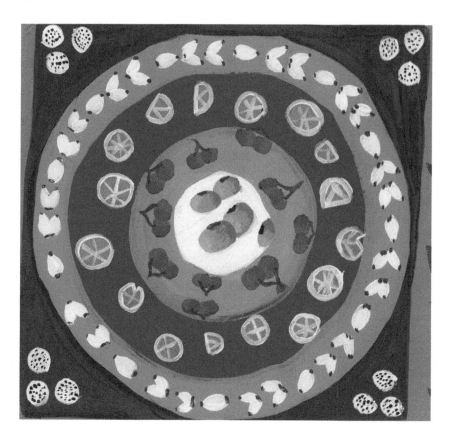

Summer: An Accordion Poem
Kyra Alway and Paolo Bosques-Paulet

I long for days of pool floaties and
sun rays dancing through the air, looking for a moment
The heavy trees and sunken clouds, slick with summer heat

Sun shining bright against our eyes
A glimmer in their reflection as the waves roll into the
tide, come in, come out
Sky hues of pink and purple shift and change, like the fluidity within
me.
Fluidity within me

Can you see me in you?
Share what we have, learn what we share
Learn the knowledge passed on from the people who pass through me
Giving me guidance in hopes of being
Free

A flashback to good times, to fond
memories to hold, in our gentle hands
Held close

Rosa Parks
Isabella Garcia Figueroa

Remove your hands from my mouth
You can't silence me

Do you hear that
People are gathering in the streets

Silence is what you want
But my voice is what you'll get

More and more will gather
Until you hear our cry for justice

More and more will gather
Until you stop killing the innocent

Silence is what you want
But my voice is what you'll get

This fight will be long
But don't worry about me

My feet might tire
yet I won't give up

Silence is what you want
But my voice is what you'll get

If you refuse to remove your hands
I'll just have to remove them off myself
 Do you hear that

Our protests are getting louder

Remembering My Home
Brittany Arzola

The summer before starting sixth grade, I moved to the east side of the train tracks in Tulare. I felt out of place in the white neighborhoods I had to walk past in order to get to school. There were small instances in which I would find people who looked like me. Nonetheless I was determined to find my place. I found comfort laying down at the end of the driveway at night, eyes locked towards the night above me. It probably wasn't the safest thing I could be doing for myself, but back at the age of 11, I found myself wondering how the world existed and I was determined to figure it out. My world was small before I began looking up at the sky. I would only wonder about instances as they were happening. My first thought was encapsulated by how humungous the star-filled sky was. Some nights, light pollution made me feel ignored by the universe; like why can't I see what's up there? I would lay my ears towards Earth, wondering if I could hear the heartbeat of Earth and the snores of those buried underneath, but was met with silence. Whenever I would put my head underneath deep waters, I wondered if I could hear anything, but again, I was met with silence. This silence swirled around in my head, wondering why I could only hear silence in the hot dry lands which was my hometown. Everyone must've found solace in their air-conditioned homes. We were tucked away in lil' old Tulare, a place where you might find a tumbleweed bouncing through. How boring... or so I thought.

Coming into our final sections of the Radical Futures class, I found Sybil Venegas's reading, "Take Me to the River: The Photography of Laura Aguilar" to be very inspiring in how Aguilar's work changed my perception on how I view a place that offers "nothing." I was introduced to the concept, "The Edge of Nothingness" as a cultural desert when Aguilar described their feelings towards the place they come from, which was South San Gabriel, saying, "Yeah, I used to tell people I grew up on the edge of nothingness!" (Venegas, 10) When reading this, I came to my roommate Jess with questions about how she felt about her experience growing up in Tulare. She also agreed with Aguilar's sentiment. We both grew up wanting more experiences that were different from what we grew up knowing. The way that

Venegas looked further beyond this edge of nothingness and found the rich cultural history of Aguilar was enlightening. I found myself wanting to do the same.

Before the late 18th century, there used to be an entire lake covering 570 sq mi of the Central Valley. It was once known as the largest freshwater lake west of the Great Lakes. Tulare Lake dried up after the rivers were diverted for agricultural irrigation and municipal water uses. The Yokuts lived amongst these areas where they fished, hunted, and had their homes when the world was their oyster until settlers came and destroyed their cosmovisiones. (Preston, 33) Cosmovisiones (world-views) is the way in which a person views, experiences, and responds to the world. The Yokuts numbered at 70,000, however, I believe there were more. This area once had one of the highest regional population densities anywhere in aboriginal North America due to how rich the habitat was. (Preston, 31) To preface, I never learned any of this history. The loss of many lives, animals, and land due to colonization sits heavy on my heart as I research more of this. Understanding the history of the stolen land I was born on helps me actualize that Tulare has a life to it that we just weren't taught about.

In William L. Preston's book, "Vanishing Landscapes: Land and Life in the Tulare Basin Lake," he stated that acorns from the great valley oak were plentiful in this area and that the Yokuts "lived principally on acorns." The Tulare Basin Lake had mussels, clams, terrapin, and fresh fish living in the waters. This area was very abundant and diverse and now Tulare is a dry hot desert where remains of the lake crack the dry ground underneath. It's horrifying that colonization caused an area that once was mostly abundant and diverse into a land plagued by water droughts.

From 2nd-5th grade, all I knew were the people I grew up amongst on the west side of Tulare. My neighbors in the cul-de-sac were all children my age who I would play outside with, most of whom were brown – just like I was. One time, we saw older kids/adults fist-fighting on the sidewalk. It was concerning to us, but we just turned around and went back inside to watch Spanish cartoons. Another memory I have growing up is about when I learned a lot about making money or hustling, as my mom would call it, because we grew up with not much. I grew up playing in sports, but it cost us a lot of money buying the uniforms. For example, when I was in cheerleading, I would go around neighborhoods on the west side, knocking on doors asking the people inside if they would like to purchase candy bars for a dollar, so that I could have enough money to buy my cheerleading uniform. My mother would buy boxes of candy from costco. A lot of us on the west side didn't have much money and it was nice to have that in common because money can be a shameful topic for me. To my young self, I viewed this as a sense of community.

This brief story of my childhood leads me into a concept I learned in the reading of "Brown Commons" by José Esteban Muñoz. Munoz states, "I am drawn to the idea of a brown commons because it captures the way in which brown people's very being is always a being-in-common" (2020, 2). They go on to say that the brown commons is made of feelings, sounds, buildings, neighborhoods, environments, and the nonhuman organic life that might circulate in such an environment alongside humans, and the inorganic presences that life is very often so attached to (Munoz 2020). My thoughts about the inorganic presences that life is very often so attached to immediately pictures the hot cheetos and pepsi I often begged my mom for. We would pass by the tiny corner store on the way home from softball/cheer practice (depending on what season it was) and grab some. The brown commons of Tulare was the entire west side of the tracks. I felt safer, as a brown person, in the place where gunshots filled the night than in the white neighborhoods I would walk through to get to school.

My emotional connection to the land really has to do with which side of the train tracks I'm on. To be on the west side meant that I was upholding a legacy in which my family created. I would've gone to Mulcahy Middle School and Tulare Western High School instead of Live Oak Middle School and Tulare Union High School. I probably would have met my now roommate/best friend if I never moved. Alas, that was not the case. The east side of Tulare was the Tulare I grew up knowing. I was an outsider/newbie/Mexican to my new white peers and neighbors and I was terrified. I found solace in running cross country; where I was able to explore this land as far as my willpower would take me. While running cross country, I found out how strong I actually am. My mother and grandmother were surprised at how much I liked running for long periods of time, but I like to think of my willpower as a reflection of theirs. I come from a long line of beautiful strong women, and honestly, I had no male-figure in my life who was as strong as my mother, grandmother, and great-grandmother.

In the reading, "Secret Gardens: Rahel Aima on Maria Thereza Alves Seeds of Change," I found out how powerful seeds are. Aima states, "Those seeds are little inadvertent hitchhikers to unspool violent histories of colonialism, transnational commerce, migration, and resource extraction. They are storytellers" (Aima, 99). They are like my great-grandmother (abuelita) Carmen who came to the United States from Guadalajara, Jalisco on her way to find a better life for her family. She was met with harsh backlash because she resisted colonialism by speaking Spanish in a white man's world. My abuelita was almost kept in the Japanese internment camps that were located at the (now) Tulare Fairgrounds because she was mistaken as being of Japanese descent. Instead of being in the internment camps, she was deported back to Mexico thus forced to make another attempt to come back to plant her roots and flourish. My abuelita knew me until she passed away when I was five-years-old. I still remember speaking to her in Spanish at her little wooden house located in Goshen. I wish I had the chance to know her more.

My grandmother Esperanza was my biggest inspiration in life. I grew up hearing her stories about how hard it was to work in the fields and how she had all twelve of her children follow in suit to help her pay bills. Her connection to the land was a laborious one, as is my mothers. My mother currently works as a groundskeeper for an elementary school. I never realized how deeply connected most of my lineage was connected to the ground, specifically in Tulare.

My connection to these environments, in which Tulare envelopes, is powerful now that I understand fully the history that I come from. Although I am not five-years-old and I am not in that period of time where I moved away from everything that I knew before sixth grade started, nor am I the cross-country runner that I knew for a while in high school. I am now a 23-year-old, who wishes she knew how precious and courageous she was while growing up in a town that bored her to death. I moved so far away from home that I hardly recognize it whenever I go back during breaks. I walk around Tulare knowing that although there is silence; there's power and energy in the land that has been left over time and that in itself is the loudness I was missing.

Works Cited:

Aima, Rahel. "Secret Gardens: Rahel Aima on Maria Thereza Alves Seeds of Change."(2018). Artforum International.

Muñoz, José Esteban. (2020). "Brown Commons" in Chambers-Letson and Nyong'o (eds.), *The Sense of Brown* (2020). Duke University Press. pp.1-7.

Preston, William L. *Vanishing Landscapes: Land and Life in the Tulare Basin Lake*. (1981). University of California Press.

Venegas, Sybil. "Take Me to the River: The Photography of Laura Aguilar" in Epstein, Rebecca (ed.), *Laura Aguilar: Show and Tell* (2017). UCLA Chicano Studies Research Center Press.

Por Mi
Destiny Rodriguez

"Tú eres muy inteligente, no te preocupes."
"Tú vas a hacer muchas cosas buenas en tu vida."
Era lo que mi abuelo siempre me decía.
"Hit books, you got this kid." My dad always tells me.

Mi mamá es de México and my dad Mexican-American.
Ella me enseña mi cultura, mi sangre y el español.
My dad shows me the hard work that is behind what it takes to succeed.

Siempre en la escuela yo trataba de hacer más
porque mucha gente no pensaba que yo podría triunfar.
I wanted to be on top to prove that I am able to do both.
En Español, and in English.

Cuando pienso en mi futuro mi mamá siempre me dice:
"Te puedes quedar aquí en Eureka para ir a la escuela,"
But I want to go out and see more than just Eureka.
"Pero mamá, tú vas a ir conmigo."
She laughs.
Siempre quiero hacer más,
porque la vida es un regalo.
A seed, que crece como una gran flor.

My sister changes my perspectives
and motivates me to do good in school.
Yo quiero ser como ella,
go to school and get a degree in something I love.
She tells me
"Nadie puede darte un regalo más grande del que tú puedes darte a ti misma."

So I want to grab ahold of
my future.

Encontrar mi momento.
Always strive for more.
Enseñarle al mundo
que yo lo puedo hacer todo.
Be more
Determined,
Fearless y
Fuerte.

I want to do
all of this
For me.

Our Need for Space
Alicia Lopez

Community begins with people. Not only those who currently reside on that land put past caretakers as well. My community is between West Adams and Crenshaw in Los Angeles. It is on Chumash Tongva (Gabrielino) indigenous land. The history of the land is important to acknowledge those who have lived before you and recognize their way of life. My community members are a mix of Oaxacan and Salvadoran people. Many members of my community migrated from their homeland at a young age or after marriage, to have a better life for themselves and their children. These migrations were not easy; it took various attempts to get here (U.S.) for some. Also, leaving behind family in their homeland is not an easy task and should not be overlooked.

My community found a place of sanction and a sense of home at my local Catholic church. This is where my community resides. Within this community environment, people of different ethnic backgrounds gather such as Korean and African American individuals. We all gather and practice our religion in the same space but at different times. The dominant members of this community are Oaxacans, referring to themselves as "Zapotec or as Indigenous people (Blackwell, 162). A key example of a cultural practice we hold is the celebration of patron saint days (often several within one year). According to Blackwell, these place-making practices have led, even more recently, to the migration of the patron saints themselves (163). Yes, we often attend different celebrations for different saints at other local parishes. Performances by Oaxacan dance troupes and brass bands are also present during these events. Events such as these, provide first-generation individuals like myself a sense of identity–Mexican/Oaxacan/American. Cultural practices are being taught by the older generation and brought to life in other parts of the world, including my church.

Another place in my community that provides a sense of belonging would be the local Oaxacan bakery/restaurant/ grocery store. The name of this store is El Valle Oaxaqueño. The vibrant color of papel picado hanging from the ceiling, the smell of all the traditional food, and fresh pan de yema or yolk bread. All these elements and participating in Sunday mass make me feel at home. Sounds within my community would be the helicopter in the sky which swoops back and forth along the streets. Plus, Latin music by Juan Gabriel, Luis Miguel, Chayanne, Pedro Infante and so many more. All provide a sense of home, because they provide me with a sense of identity, and feeling of belonging. Yet, I am aware of my surroundings and the injustices occurring in the background. In my neighborhood, gentrification is a constant challenge. Many of my community members are being displaced from their homes. Moving to cheaper affordable housing, further down to East Los Angeles or leaving Los Angeles completely. This causes many of us to lose relationships that have been built over time. In addition to feeling less of a cultural community when those who move are from the same town my family is from. Displacement or migration is due to the tearing down of worn-down homes and building of tall apartment complexes.

According to Nielsen, displacement causes community members to pay disproportionately high rents due to real estate booms caused by new infrastructures, what she calls a "wave of condominium conversions" that are more aesthetically pleasing to incomers looking to rent or buy refurbished homes (Nielsen, 123-132). Incoming homeowners from suburban neighborhoods are flooding in, replacing low-income families who once lived there. She adds that these real estate booms have "drawn people to the region since the 1880s, when Union and Pacific Railroads fought to bring customers west" (Nielsen, 130). Gentrification also causes "increasing shortages of land and water and severe congestion and traffic problems" (Nielsen, 131). My family and many others have to find solutions to overpopulation in my neighborhood. One such example is having to park two or more streets down from where you live. Traffic in Los Angeles is an overwhelming challenge many Los Angelinos face in their everyday routine.

My community as well as others has its forms of resistance. My community speaks up through the use of murals. All around Los Angeles murals provide a sense of belonging and honor. For instance, artist Noni Olabisi and her mural "To Protect and to Serve" on Jefferson Boulevard and 11th Avenue, "was one of the first murals to address the history of police brutality" (Gutiérrez, 2022). "I wanted the wall to scream," said Noni Olabisi regarding this piece. Her mural brought to light the subject of police brutality, racial discrimination, educational inequalities, access to health care, food insecurity, and all rights Black Panthers strived for, alongside the Brown Berets. This mural is my community's form of resistance and its continued demand for change as well as a "homage to Black radical organizing embodied by Huey Newton, Angela Davis and other members of the Black Panthers" (Gutiérrez, 2022).

Murals are marks to acknowledge our history, the history of community members, and their unforgotten past. They are footprints left even if we the community are displaced and no

longer reside there – pushed out due to gentrification, our footprints stay. African American and Latina/o relations and interaction highlight "the struggle of both communities, collectively and separately, for dignity, strength, and solidarity against all the odds" (Rosas, 101). "Black residents... worked to create opportunity in the midst of the most dehumanizing forms of class, gender, and racial oppression and inequality" (Rosas, 103). This struggle is viewed through murals and other artworks of Noni Olabisi, who recently passed. Yet her work will continue to live and validate the experiences African Americans faced over time.

My family passes down our history through storytelling and photographs. My parents retell stories of their childhood back in Mexico and folktales from their childhood as well. I love listening to their stories and learning about them and the environment they grew up in. Through storytelling, I know my parents' journey coming to the United States along with the struggles they faced along the way. Although they might not give me the full context of their journey to the U.S. due to not wanting to recall a traumatic experience, I at least know part of the story and am grateful for their sharing. History is passed down through generations in various forms, such as cultural traditions, murals, storytelling, or photographs. We can acknowledge and validate those experiences by sharing our history and the history of others too.

Noni Olabisi, To Protect and Serve, 1996.
South Central Los Angeles
Photo by Alicia Lopez, 2022.

Works Cited:

Blackwell, M. "Geographies of Indigeneity: Indigenous Migrant Women's Organizing and Translocal Politics of Place." *Latino Studies*, 15.2, (2017): 156–181.

Gutiérrez, R. "Muralist Noni Olabisi, Whose Art Galvanized South Los Angeles communities, Dies at 67." *LA Times*, 8 March 2022. Retrieved November 29, 2022.

https://www.latimes.com/entertainment-arts/story/2022-03-07/muralist-noni-olabisi-los-angeles-death

Nielsen, J.T. "Immigration and the Low-Cost Housing Crisis: The Los Angeles Area's Experience." *Population and Environment*, 11.2, (1989): 123–139.

Rosas, A. *South Central Is Home: Race and the Power of Community Investment in Los Angeles*. (2019). Stanford University Press.

No Effect on Me
Brenda Santos

I have lost that side of me …
the side that lets you bring me down.
the side that lets your words affect me
I am strong
I am myself
I am all that I can be
I know myself
I know your words do not,
Define me.

Mis Motivadores
Eduardo A. Moreno-Ortiz

In my life I have had two different people that have impacted my life with their wisdom and they are my dad and my mom. When I was a child, my mom would tell me "Mijo pon atención cuando te habla la maestra." I didn't do well in school, I would either not do the homework or I would just lie to her when she asked me if I did good that day. My mind was always on soccer and how I just wanted to fulfill my childhood dream. During class, I wouldn't do the work and would talk with my friends in the back of the room. Although I would put her through a lot of stress during my years of elementary, middle, and high school my mom would still push me and force me to do great.

After my first two years of high school, I was sent to a continuation school where I would end up needing to recover 30 classes in about two years. My junior year wasn't productive at all. I only finished three classes out of the thirty and it was looking like I wasn't going to graduate. My mom found out and just yelled and cried to me. This motivated me and I came into my senior year with a chip on my shoulder. My mom got surgery at the beginning of the year. My dad was the one that started taking me to school. Every morning my dad would tell me "Try to get as many classes as you can today" and I would be even more motivated to prove that anything was possible with my hard work and dedication. I would work on the weekends with my dad and cousin in both of their businesses and I knew that I had to at least get fifteen classes done the first semester. I got seven classes done in the first semester and had to go into the second semester with eighteen classes left. I finished the last of those classes a week before graduation and was able to walk the stage.

When I graduated, my mom was able to finally be happy because I had finished a task that nobody thought I was going to accomplish. I was able to take all the stress off of my shoulders too. This past thanksgiving my dad and I were both talking outside of my uncle's house and we were looking up to the stars and he asked me what I thought when I looked up and I told him "I don't know dad I just feel peaceful when I do" he then told me "You should start thinking that you'll bright more than them" and that's what has been motivating me to be great in my freshman year at university.

¡Viva México!

Diego Vega and Georgina Cerda Salvarrey

Yo soy de mi familia por el apoyo
Yo soy de mis padres por el amor
Yo soy de mis primos por el cariño
Yo soy de la lucha por alzar mi voz

Yo soy del folk de Ed Maverick y Daniel Quién
Yo soy del indie por lo que siento
Yo soy de rock en español
Entonces yo soy de la música de corazón

Yo soy de la comida porque es lo mejor
Yo soy de las enchiladas por el auténtico sabor
Yo soy de los tacos por el sazón
Yo soy del elote pa' mí y del esquite pa' ti

¡NOSOTROS SOMOS DE MÉXICO!

I Am Who I Am
Claudia Lopez-Hernandez

I am who I am
Who decided to consider people a label?
They call them rich.
They call them poor.
They see the rich as white.
They see the poor as brown and black
But who are they to judge
someone they have never met?

Yo soy quien yo soy
a pesar de mi color de piel
o lo que ellos piensen de mí.

Growing up as a Mexican/American girl
had its ups and downs.
I often got judged
everywhere I went
for the way I looked.

Estando en México
no me siento suficientemente mexicana,
pero aquí no me siento suficientemente americana.
No hablo bien el español estando en México,
pero tampoco hablo bien el inglés estando aquí.

I am who I am despite my color
and
your judgments.

I am
Kyra Alway

I am a question, a promise
A certainty of accomplishment
A "you will be successful"
I am the smartest in the room
I am the mental math, the six-year-old who calculated the tip
I am "mature for your age" and a "future honors student"

I am pressured, I am small
I was so focused on who to become
I don't know who I am anymore.
I am "pretty", I am "beautiful"
I am a bird on display
With my fake shiny feathers and my lovely little song

But I am underneath that image,
my song is only a voice box
Repeating the same lost tune
Can you hear me?

I want a voice
To say
"I CRY", "I LIVE"
"I AM HUMAN", "LET ME BE"
And I am finding it
My arms are growing
My feathers now wings
I am an answer.

Here We Stand

Nelsy Ramirez Pacheco and Chelsea Rios Gomez

We are from migration
De los que sacrificaron everything they knew
From leaving behind family, language, and land
In which our roots grow

Somos de respeto y amor
De unidad y dolor
De sacrificios hechos por generación

We are from new opportunities
Of labor and educación

De cultura Mexicana
Where our pride flows
Dónde familia es lo primero
Con confianza que siempre permanecen

Estamos aquí
Whether you like it or not.

From Roots to Wings
Anonymous, Anonymous

From the rolling hills of Pennsylvania
To the smog filled city of LA
To winding rivers and long stretches of rural coastline

From a broken home, with hearts still full
From an estranged family, still full of love
From mi familia rooted in connections
As strong as the Redwoods around us
Like the instinct of the chinook
Our inner compass guided us home

Like the monarch in the spring
We have morphed and spread our wings
From the collective Rio de la Vida
Our streams diverge

Yet I've learned all paths of water lead to the ocean
And here we are conectados
Even though we've grown in different places
We are all familiar faces
For we gaze at the same moon, bask in the same sunlight
Y respiramos el mismo aire

El Primer Dia
Erick Esparza

Mi primer día en la escuela,
caminé hacia una silla
cuando escuché:
"What is your name?"
¿Qué? No entiendo.
In my head
I kept wondering:
¿Qué están diciendo?
Kids surrounded me,
they kept repeating:
"What is your name?"
¿Qué? No entiendo, I said.
I could feel their eyes
glaring at me.
It was difficult to breathe.
I was scared
alone.
Unable to respond
Only murmuring to them,
"No entiendo."

I remember
going home and
asking my mom:

¿Por qué soy diferente?

Nopayele
Cayele Ameyalli Esteva

Being Part of the LGBTQ+ Community
Genevive Cerda

As you may know, being part of the LGBTQ+ community is not a choice, it is simply who somebody is. It can be hard enough for someone of the community to "come out" to their loved ones. Being born into a religious family and/or household can add a lot of pressure to this. Not only might they be going against their family's belief systems, but they are fearful of losing their loved ones simply because of who they are. In many cases, homosexuality of any kind is considered shameful and a sin. Growing up in a religious household also means traditions which includes learning how a traditional family should appear to the public and how they should act. However, there are also instances where to some, having a loving family is all that matters. Although a lot of people don't mind homosexuality, it might still be "forbidden" to older generations. Another hardship the community faces is having to be careful living their day-to-day lives because there are also non-religious people who also find homosexuality to be wrong. Homophobia is similar to racism in the sense that both things are taught and nobody is born with hatred towards somebody that has no control over their sexuality or the color of their skin. Although there might be more support of the LGBTQ+ community now than there used to be, we still face daily discrimination because of our sexualities. Luckily, I was born with a mom who has made it clear that she and her side of the family accept and support anyone in the community. However, I am not out to my family yet because I still consider it difficult, especially since my father's side is more conservative, traditional, and religious. This affects me because it makes me feel as if I'm an outsider in my home and as much as I love my family, growing up in that environment of what they consider to be the right and wrong ways of living make me feel unimportant, unseen, and unheard; it makes me wonder if their love for me would change and if they would try to "make me straight." I cannot speak for everyone, but not being able to share how you feel to the people you grew up with and love could make you feel isolated and alone. Although you might not be able to "change" someone's perspective on certain things, bringing the situation(s) to light and educating people would definitely make a difference. If we sat down and took the time to educate ourselves on these topics, there might be change sooner rather than later.

Querida Niña
Georgina Cerda Salvarrey

Querida niña
Se que has pasado por mucho
Que eres sensible y vulnerable
Que la mirada ajena te aprieta el pecho
Dejando escasez y vacío inefable

La realidad te alcanza cuando te olvidas de tu alma
Un alma imperfecta como las piedras del río
No te condenes por ser diferente,
no te compares con las demás piedras

La belleza debajo del caudaloso hastío
No repara en los gritos del mundo
El mundo quiere todo perfecto
Se tu quien lo niega y abraza tu poderío.

Aunque te encuentres en tierra lejana
Perdonate mi niña y sana
Deja que el fresco viento renueve tu brío
Que eres valiosa y sagrada montaña

This is Me
Kimberly Piñon

People just assume,
form their thoughts
give their opinions
about people
based on
past experiences.

People have perceived me
as shy, loud, respectful, disrespectful, reckless, responsible, kind,
mean, helpless, etc.

When in reality I am funny, awkward, tough, angry, sad, happy,
tired, exhausted, desperate, helpful, brutally honest, reckless, patient,
impatient, peaceful, brave, cowardly, aggressive, but most of all I am
unbroken and strong.

I have lived through things I never thought were going to happen to
me and have learned from them but I am not healed so I remain caged
with emotions.

I do not let on what I am feeling because I am self-reliant and don't
ask for help unless necessary.

I am resourceful so I know whatever I want I will get which makes
me determined but strong headed.

I am confused about what I want for my future which is utterly terrifying.

I have many emotions going on in my head at every moment and they
are all fighting and struggling with each other but on the exterior, I
can handle it all. It's when I am alone that it all consumes me, but I
know I will be okay.

The Language of English
Sasha Ortiz Bazan

I always hated my parent's broken English, with stumbles upon stumbles. I remember eyes staring, whispers all around, pity in people's eyes. I HATED It! I never realized how much I hated it, until I started growing up and started noticing the judgmental stares.

All I remember as a 13-year-old teenager is only caring about friendships and makeup.

But even though my parents spoke broken English, they always communicated with such joyful pride. There was no shame about the way that their English came across to others. They didn't seem to care at all. I constantly questioned them, "Aren't you embarrassed? Aren't you scared about what others think?" They responded with pride:

"Y porque deberíamos avergonzarnos!"

But why did I never realize the beauty in their voice? The efforts they made to give me a better life? A life they never had, the one they always wished for us.

I realize now that I was ignorant and immature.

But I see it now, the beauty of my roots and how deep they grow. I now feel pride and am able to vigorously support my culture, their struggles and accomplishments.

So, Mama and Papa thank you for instilling pride about where I came from. Thank you for making me realize the worth of things that I took for granted. I know I have a lot of growing up to do, but at least I know I won't be alone, and no matter what we will always be connected. So, like you always tell me, "te amo hasta la luna y las estrellas."

Con mucho amor tu princesa y tu luz,

Sasha O

The Hieroglyph

The hieroglyph (glyph) artwork was created by Michael Tjoelker, a student at Humboldt State University in 2016.

The glyph is inspired by Nahuatl hieroglyphs used by the Aztecs in Mesoamerica. The single glyph, tlatoa, denotes speech, important speech, speech spoken by individuals who held social, political, or religious positions of power and thus justified the writing of their speech.

This Journal reclaims the glyph to foreground the power of speech, the assertion that students already possess important knowledge, and the primacy of telling their cuentos — of telling their stories.

By orienting four glyphs towards a center we intend it to mean that the CouRaGeouS Cuentos in this journal are a form of liberatory dialogue worthy of writing and publishing. Importantly, it is a conversation within community.

Volume 6 Poster

Strawberry Mango Paletas
Recipe by Brianna R. Juarez

Ingredients:
- 12 strawberries
- 2 mangoes
- 1 ½ lemons
- 2 cups of ice
- Chirris rebanaditas (Watermelon chile candies)
- Chamoy
- Tajin
- Mango nectar

Prep:
- Wash and chop strawberries & set aside
- Wash, peel, and chop mangoes & set aside
- Squeeze the juice of 1 ½ lemons or limes & set aside
- Roughly blend approximately 7 candies & set aside

Instructions:
- To a blender: add ice, mangoes, half of the squeezed lemon juice, mango nectar & blend to a puree & set aside.
- To a clean blender: add ice, strawberries, remainder of lemon juice, chamoy & blend to a puree & set aside.
- To your popsicle molds: add some tajin, blended candy, chamoy & swish it around to spread the mixture.
- Next, add some strawberry puree then mango puree on each mold and repeat until all the molds are filled.
- Add some more blended candies, chamoy, & tajin.
- Lastly, allow to freeze for 6 hours to overnight. Enjoy!

Find a step-by-step tutorial on our Instagram page:
@courageouscuentos

Author Bios

ADRIAN VIELMA GARCIA (he/him), author of "Sueños/Dreams" is from Escondido, CA and is 17 years old. He is interested in majoring in psychology because of the impact it can have on a community. Disfruto salir con mis amigos y tocar la guitarra en mi tiempo libre.

ALICIA LOPEZ (she/her) author of "Our Need for Space" is from Los Angeles, California. She is majoring in Liberal Studies Child Development Elementary Education (LSCE). She loves dogs, cats and all furry creatures. She enjoys doing arts and crafts on her free time and spending quality time with her family and friends.

ANAYKA FLORES (she/her), autor de "Cambios en 1...2 por 3" es de Lima, Perú. Para Anayka, no fue fácil llegar a este país ni tampoco aprender el idioma, pero al final logro aprender los dos idiomas a la perfección.

ANDREA ITZEL VELAZCO QUIROZ (her/she), autor de "Dejar Todo Sin Dejar Nada" es de Morelia Michoacán, México. Nació en Los Banos, California, y se mudó de 3 años a México. Tiene 17 años y regreso a los 16 a los EE.UU. Lo que más disfruta y cree que es parte de ella es la música—escucharla, y crearla.

ANILU RODRIGUEZ (she/her), autor de "Mi Lugar Favorito" nació en Los Angeles y creció en México. Le gusta intentar cosas nuevas y disfrutar de los placeres de la vida.

ANITZA MONARREZ (she/her/ella) is author of "Necesidad y Sacrificio: San Ysidro, Su Frontera, y Su Gente." She was born in Tijuana, moved to the USA in 2011 at the age of 10 and has lived in San Ysidro, CA ever since. She enjoys art and storytelling. Mi nombre es Anitza Rocio Monarrez Valdez, soy nacida en Tijuana, criada Sinaloense. Emigre a los Estados Unidos a la edad de 10 años y he vivido en San Ysidro, CA desde entonces. Me gusta el arte y compartir historias.

ANONYMOUS (they/them), is the artist of the portrait "Walnuts." They are from the Santa Cruz Mountains and is a studio art major at Humboldt. They enjoy ceramics, dancing, and being in nature. Most of their time is spent creating by themselves or with their friends.

ARIANNA BUCIO (she/her), author of "Ama" is a critical race, gender, & sexuality studies major. She is passionate about supporting Black & Brown communities to encourage the overall physical, mental, and spiritual well-being of one another. She tries to make constant efforts to decolonize my life and education to help create avenues of growth within my own community.

AUDRIANA PEÑALOZA (she/her), author of "Four-Leafed Clovers" is from the Central Valley; originally grew up in Arvin, CA. She is expected to graduate with her Bachelor's degree in English in the spring of 2023. She plans to attend grad school shortly after where she will continue to learn more about English and Ethnic Studies and how they can work together.

BELLA FIGUEROA (she/her), author of "Rosa Parks" is from Healdsburg, California. She is currently a freshman majoring in Kinesiology with hopes of becoming a physical therapist. She enjoys spending time outdoors or with animals.

BENJAMIN CROSS (he/him) is author of "The Maidu and Miwok People in the Wake of California's "Growth"." He is from Auburn, California and is majoring in Political Science with a focus on the environment and sustainability, and is expected to graduate spring of 2023. In learning, he is always at his happiest when he can interact with different perspectives than his own. Similarly, any time he can spend in nature is far from wasted time in his mind.

BRENDA SANTOS (she/her/hers), author of "No Effect on Me" is majoring in early elementary education.

BRIANNA R. JUAREZ (she/her), author of "Understanding My New Normal" is a senior philosophy major with a minor in comparative ethnic studies. She is also a part of the Courageous Cuentos 2023 social media team and loves it.

BRITTANY "BROT" ARZOLA (They/Them), author of "Remembering my Home" is from Yokut territory located in the Central Valley. They are majoring in CRGS - Ethnic Studies and minoring in American Indian Education. They enjoy karaoking with friends, cooking, and crocheting.

CARMEN BENAVIDES-GARB (She/Her), is author of "Gracias a Dios." She is from Humboldt County and currently studying abroad in Spain. She is a double major in CRGS and Political Science with a minor in Spanish. She really enjoys traveling and hopes her readers enjoy/resonate with her piece.

CARMEN SAHAGUN (she/her), author of "enough" is from Hollister, California. She will be graduating in 2023 with a BS in Environmental Science & Management with a concentration in Education and Interpretation. She enjoys connecting with nature and helping others (particularly children) to do the same, especially in historically underrepresented BIPOC communities with less opportunity and equitable access to nature recreation.

CAYELE AMEYALLI ESTEVA (he/they), is the artist of the self-portrait "Nopayele." He is from Oakland, majoring in Tribal Forestry. With this piece he wanted to show his thoughts on growing up in a Mexican family and not being able to fluently speak Spanish to communicate with all of his family.

CHELSEA RIOS GOMEZ (they/them/elle), co-author of "Here We Stand" and author of "Ode to the One That Raised Me" is from the occupied, unceded indigenous land of the Yokuts. They are a psychology major, who enjoys learning and questioning the systems in which we exist.

CHRISTO SANTIAGO (He/Him), author of "Nuestros Pasos en algo Diferente" is from Bakersfield, CA. He is a history major and enjoys the way in which it encourages him to explore and understand new events and occurrences. He is always eager to spend time with his family describing this as "a place that keeps me happy and motivates me to keep on going.

CLAUDIA LOPEZ-HERNANDEZ (she/her), author of "I Am Who I am" is from Bakersfield, CA. She is a high school student at Eureka High School. She enjoys spending time with her family.

COVIN SIGALA (they/them) artist of the self-portrait "Basil & Rose" is from Salinas, California. They are double majoring in Environmental Science and Wildlife with a minor in Indigenous Peoples, Natural Resource Use, and the Environment. They drew themselves with basil to represent their mom's mother and a rose to represent their dad's mother.

DAVIS BOONE (he/him), co-author of "Somos Musicos" is from Eureka, California. He hopes to major in a science or medical subject, while continuing to play the violin.

DESTINY RODRIGUEZ (she/her), author of "Por Mi" is from Eureka, CA. She plans on going to a CSU or UC and she plans on studying and pursuing a career in the medical field.

DIEGO VEGA (him/he), co-autor de "Viva México" es de la Ciudad de México. Tiene 17 años. Le gusta mucho la música y transmitir con ella todo lo que siente. Le gusta dibujar y le gustan los deportes en especial el basketball.

DILLON AVERY HARP (he/him) is author of "Our People." He is a CRGS/Ethnic Studies major and is working on his Master's degree in Environment and Community concurrently. He was born in Galveston, TX (Home of Juneteenth) and is unapologetically Black and proud. He is also a Musician/Producer/Composer and Poet/MC/Writer. He loves traveling, cooking and eating spicy food.

EDUARDO A. MORENO-ORTIZ (he/him), author of, "Mis Motivadores" was born and raised in Los Angeles. He is majoring in Kinesiology with a concentration in pre-med.

EMMANUEL CARO MONTOYA (he/him), author of "Aprender a Vivir" is from Sinaloa, Mexico. He is currently a student at Eureka High School. He enjoys watching soccer (fútbol).

ERICK ESPARZA (He/Him), author of "What is your name" resides in Eureka, California. He is of Mexican background and enjoys 1v1ing.

GENEVIVE CERDA (she/her), author of "Being Part of the LGBTQ+ Community" is from San Diego, California and majoring in liberal studies. She enjoys reading in her free time and hanging out with friends.

GEORGINA "GINA" CERDA SAVARREY (she/her), Mexicana de este lado, es autora de "Querida Nina", "Unlearn", y "Miedo" y co-autor de "Viva México" es de Monterrey. Le gusta leer, escribir, trabajar en solidaridad y pasar mucho tiempo en la naturaleza.

GERBER CAMPOS, autor de "La Madrugada Amarga" nació en Guatemala. Le gusta jugar soccer y ir al gimnasio y lo que más disfruta es jugar y hacer ejercicio.

GREGORIO MUNIZ (he/him), author of "Gregorio Muniz (x3)" is from Orange County, CA. He is a Critical Race, Gender & Sexuality Studies major with a pathway in Ethnic Studies and a minor in Ethnic American Literature. He enjoys cooking, spending time with his dog, and going on adventures.

GRISELDA VALDEZ (she/her), co-author of "Miedo" is a first-generation college student and is majoring in Environmental Science and Management. She loves going on nature walks and living in Humboldt County.

HALEY FEDALIZO (they/them/elle), co-author of "The Aftermath of Absence" is on the path to be a Life Science Educator that advocates for equitable and inclusive curriculum. They are focused on empowering BIPOC & LGBTQ+ youth.

HANSELL VÁSQUEZ (el), es autor de "Deseo Poder Conocerte." Su nombre completo es Hansell Yohaly Vasquez Moran y es de Guatemala. Le gusta escuchar música y en sus tiempos libres le gusta estar solo.

HUNTER CIRCE (he/him) is author of "My Mother the Spider." He grew up in Humboldt County and is majoring in Environmental

Studies. You can find him in the darkness of a movie theater, corner of a bar, or out eating oysters somewhere.

ISABELA ESCOBEDO (she/they), author of "Radical Futures" is from Seattle, WA, majoring in Critical Race, Gender, and Sexuality Studies. She loves taking her dog for long walks and painting with her outside.

JESSE MORALES (they/them) is the artist of the self-portrait "Untitled (Mess No. 1)." They are from the greater Sacramento area, majoring in Fine Arts. Their focus is ceramics and using majolica and Talavera art to inspire their forms, but they enjoy creation in all forms.

JESSICA AGUIRRE (she/her) author of "agua bendita" is from Tulare, California. She is majoring in Critical Race, Gender & Sexuality Studies, specifically Ethnic Studies. Le dedicó este pasaje a mi mamá y papa y a todos mis hermano/as. Los quiero mucho <3

JOAHNNA TOOL (she/her/they), author of "Descubriendo" and they are a social work major and a Spanish minor. She enjoys listening to music, photography, and spending time in nature.

JORDAN LAVANT (she/her), co-author of "The Aftermath of Absence" is a mixed-race student (black and white) originally from Virginia, but moved to California when she was 13. She is 17 at the time of writing this, and finishing her senior year at Eureka High School. She plans to attend San José State University to major in psychology to hopefully become a criminal profiler.

JOSE MACEDA, autor de "Mi Recuerdo Inolvidable" tiene 18 años, y es de México. Le gusta estudiar y le gusta jugar basketball.

KACIE E. FIGUEROA (she/they), author of "Chicana, Para El Norte" is from Riverbank, CA. She is majoring in Critical Race, Gender, and Sexuality Studies with a pathway in Ethnic Studies. She enjoys being around loved ones and drawing her small creatures.

KAREN ZURITA (they/she) is author of "I am Not Afraid." They grew up in the San Fernando Valley and is currently working on finishing their masters in Literary and Cultural studies at Cal Poly Humboldt.

They want to dedicate their poem to first-generation Xicanx students that sometimes feel lost when writing. They hope this poem reminds you that our writing is sacred and alive.

KATHRYN LOZANO (she/her) is the artist of the self-portrait "Mejillas Rosadas." She is studying political science here at Cal Poly Humboldt. She has learned new things about herself and others in this magical place among the trees and ocean, much different than her hometown of Fullerton, CA.

KATHY ZAMORA (she/her/ella), author of "Kathy Pero Like Katí" es hija de Revocata Escamilla Mendez y Modesto Zamora Vasquez. Está estudiando trabajo social, y en mayo 2023 se graduará. Va a continuar con su maestría este año en trabajo social. Está manifestando que un día obtendrá su doctorado/PhD en estudios étnicos o estudios de chicano/x.

KENA ARNOLD-MALUFAU (they/them), author of "A Testimony Denouncing Religion" is an English Education major. Writing is one of their forms of self-expression, specifically poetry. They always hope that their writing is relatable to others to keep everyone connected.

KIMBERLI PACHECO (she/her), author of "Where am I from?" is from Eureka, Ca. In the future, she hopes to be a lawyer and help those in need. She enjoys rainy days and swimming in the river with her family.

KIMBERLY PIÑON (she/her), author of "This is Me" is a Kinesiology major with an emphasis in Exercise Science. She enjoys playing tennis, hiking, swimming, and spending time with her six dogs. También me encanta escribir y hablar español, aunque no lo haga enfrente de mis compañeros. Pero I really enjoyed writing my testimonio for my Creando Raíces class this semester.

KIMBERLYN RAMIREZ MORENO (she/her), author of "Agradecida" is 17 years old. She is from Eureka, CA.

KYRA ALWAY (she/her), co-author of "Summer: An Accordion Poem" and author of "I Am" is from Arcata High School in Humboldt

County, a small town in Northern California. She is a junior in high school and she was super excited for the chance to work with Cal Poly Humboldt students to create this poem. She enjoys listening to music and hanging out with her family, and she is super grateful for this opportunity!

LESLIE BURKHART (she/her) is the artist of the self-portrait "Leslie & Poppy." She is majoring in Environmental Ed and Interpretation, with minors in German and Botany this summer. Poppy flowers symbolize my state and are a delightful mass of color on roadsides and spring hillsides. Her family, the Papaveraceae, also have delighted and surprised me; they appear bright red in Tasmania's neatly fenced fields of opium, and incomprehensively blue in the midnight light in Iceland's Botanic Garden.

LOGAN ROSELLI (he/him) author of "How Riverside County Celebrates Historical Indigenous Oppression" is from Riverside, CA. He is a business major at Cal Poly Humboldt with a concentration in New Venture Management. He looks forward to using my degree to create and support environmentally-focused businesses.

LUIS CAMACHO GARCIA (El), autor de "Dejar a mis Padres" es nacido en Eureka, California y criado en Ciudad Obregón, Sonora. Le gusta asistir su escuela secundaria para convivir con sus amigos. En su tiempo libre disfruta de la playa.

LUIS EDUARDO RODRIGUEZ (he/him), author of "Una Vida Sin Mamá Ni Hermanos" is from Nayarit, Mexico. He enjoys playing soccer and baseball.

LUIS FRANCISCO MARTÍNEZ, autor de "Dejando Todo" es de un pueblito que se llama San Martin Itunyoso. Le gustaría estudiar para ser doctor y poder ayudar a las personas de su pueblo. Disfruta tocar la guitarra y le gustaría tocar con su ídolo algún día.

MARCO ANTONIO CRUZ HERNANDEZ (he/him), author of "Medicina" is from Eureka, California. He enjoys playing football and playing videogames and spending time with his family.

MARIA CITLALLI RODRIGUEZ (she/they), is author of "Our Connection." She moved around quite a bit as a kid, but she always felt at home as long as she was with my family. They offer protection and love which is something she wants to share with others. She loves being creative whether that be making art or writing. She spent the majority of her educational journey in San Bernardino, but currently resides in the vast landscape of the High Desert. Humboldt is a wonderful opposite with cool breezes highlighted with sunny days.

MARISOL RUIZ (she/ her) is a professor in the School of Education at Cal Poly Humboldt where she teaches courses to prepare future social justice-oriented teachers in the K-12 classroom. She grew up in the San Francisco Mission District but with gentrification she was pushed to North Oakland. She is the proud daughter of a refugee mother from Chile. She grew up in an all women household with abuelita, mom, and two younger sisters. When she thinks of paletas she is reminded of the best paleteria ever which was located in the heart of 24th street Mission District. There, paletas were made by hand with fresh fruits. She was devastated when the family business closed their doors. She has yet to taste a paleta as good as theirs. Today her favorite paletas are coco rallado, sandia , and pepino con chile.

MATT AUNG (he/him), author of "The Puzzle of Me" and "Naypyidaw" and co-author of "Places We're From" is a triple major studying Art History, Art Education, and Art Studio. He is also studying for his gallery and museum certificate and he hopes to be an art educator in the future.

MAYRA MEZA (them/they), co-author of "Somos Musicos" and "Miedo" is from East Los Angeles majoring in Music Education. They have been learning the violin for the last 7 years training with top notch violinists in Los Angeles. On their free time, they like to bike ride, fish, disc golfing and hiking.

MELISSA TORRES ESCALANTE (she/they), author of "Para Mi Papa, Que Sigue Viviendo en el Mar" is from Orange County, and is majoring in Psychology. What she enjoys in her free time is listening to music, going on drives through Humboldt County, and for whatever reason signing up for presentations in her other classes. She is a Latine, first-gen student and her goal is to uplift her community by entering academia and doing work that focuses on highlighting the unique experiences that the Latine community goes through.

MIA ROSE RIOS (she/they) author of "My Garden" is from Tulare, CA. This is her second year here at Cal Poly Humboldt as a Liberal Studies Elementary Education major. Her writing is about the struggle and growth she experienced when she first moved to Humboldt out of high school as a Mexican American and how much of a positive impact people she has made connections with motivate her.

MINERVA TORRES (they/them) is the artist of the self-portrait "Body is Soil, Hair is Flower." Minerva has lived in too many places to "be" from any of them, but is trying to one day find a place to call home. They enjoy history, fashion and storytelling. They hope to do something with those in the future.

MIRIAM RODRIGUEZ, autor de "Una Vida Sin Mi Mamá en Otro País" nació en los estados unidos pero mis padres son de México. Le gusta estudiar geometry y disfruta mucho la clase de spanish.

NAMIXTU'LÚ' ESTEVA (she/they) is the artist of the self-portrait "Xelfi." She is a first-year student majoring in Environmental Studies. She enjoys being creative and one thing that's important to her is implementing the knowledge of her ancestors and teachings of her elders into all of her projects and work that she does.

NANCY PÉREZ (she/her) is an assistant professor in the Critical Race, Gender & Sexuality Studies Department at Cal Poly Humboldt where she teaches courses in Ethnic Studies. She grew up in Boyle Heights, CA and is a proud daughter of immigrant parents from Zacatecas, Mexico. She enjoys watching art and music documentaries, going to punk rock shows, drinking coffee, and spending time with her furry companion Chimichanga.

NAYALI ABARCA-RUIZ (she/her) is a Studio Arts major at San Diego State University. She graduated from Six Rivers High School in 2017. After graduating from Six Rivers, she went to Skyline Community College where she graduated with her Cosmetology Degree and an

Associate Degree in Studio Art. After receiving her Associate Degree, she transferred to San Diego State University where she is pursuing a Bachelor's Degree in Studio Art. Her hobbies include ceramics, jewelry making, painting and photography.

NELSY RAMIREZ PACHECO (she/her), co-author of "Here We Stand" was born and raised in Eureka, California. She is a junior at Eureka High School. She enjoyed writing along with Chelsea Rios Gomez because they got to express their Mexican culture through writings which was very delightful. They are working hard in school to make their parents proud.

NOEMI GONZALEZ MALDONADO (she/her/ella), author of "Silencio" is a first-generation high school and college graduate. For Noemi, home is 5 hrs. away in an agricultural town by the name of Watsonville. The Killer Klowns from Outer space was filmed there. She is on her second year of graduate school under the Applied English Master program. Her focus and interest lay in the preservation of native languages, as well as stepping away from colonial languages like Spanish and English. She aims to dismantle the notion that being able to speak Spanish correctly makes you more or less Mexican.

OLIE M. ESPINOZA (they/he), is the artist of the self-portrait "Rooted Home." They are from Colton, CA and majoring in environmental science with an eco resto concentration. They enjoy eating fruits, adventures, music, and writing.

PAOLO BOSQUES-PAULET (he/him), co-author of "Summer: An Accordion Poem" is a Junior at Arcata High School. He likes cashews, wrestling, and going to the beach. They had fun and enriching experience being a part of the Promotorx Transformative Educators Workshop.

RIVER JUDE RUIZ (he/him) is the artist of the self-portrait "Principe de Aloe." He is a Poli-Sci Major with a concentration in Law & Policy. He is from East L.A and grew up in Yuba City, CA. He loves to ride horses and play video games and is working to become a Lawyer.

SASHA ORTIZ BAZAN (her/she), author of "The Language of English" is from Eureka, but her parents are from Michigan. What she wants to major in is Bachelor of Science in Nursing. She enjoys hanging out with friends and watching anime/manga, especially *One Piece* and *Eyeshield 21* which both define her childhood memories.

SKY KILI (they/them), is from PA and they are majoring in Environmental Studies. They love to rock climb and surf with their friends and backpack with their dog.

SYDNEY LELAND (she/they), author of "Be Proud and Loud" is from upstate New York. She is a transfer student majoring in Psychology. She enjoys people pleasing and making others happy.

TIM OLSON (his/him/he), author of "Mis Placas Tectonicas" is a teacher of Spanish for the past 27 years. He enjoys his job, especially working with heritage speakers. He feels like he can make a positive difference in their lives.

YAMI E.P.M (she/her), autor de "Locked" es de Eureka, CA. Le gusta comer y dormir y disfruta mirar películas Korean.

Why CouRaGeouS Cuentos?

Courageous Cuentos represents a revolutionary platform that offers
Cal Poly Humboldt's diverse student body a safe and supportive
space to express their unique voices in languages that uplift their
ancestral truths. As an annual publication led exclusively by students,
the journal, its associated class, and book launch party has become
a cultural staple on our campus that fosters student's exploration of
their personal ethno-cultural narratives.

Made in the USA
Coppell, TX
16 July 2023

19208558R00105